OECD Sovereign Borrowing Outlook
2020

OECD

BETTER POLICIES FOR BETTER LIVES

This work is published under the responsibility of the Secretary-General of the OECD. The opinions expressed and arguments employed herein do not necessarily reflect the official views of OECD member countries.

This document, as well as any data and map included herein, are without prejudice to the status of or sovereignty over any territory, to the delimitation of international frontiers and boundaries and to the name of any territory, city or area.

The statistical data for Israel are supplied by and under the responsibility of the relevant Israeli authorities. The use of such data by the OECD is without prejudice to the status of the Golan Heights, East Jerusalem and Israeli settlements in the West Bank under the terms of international law.

Please cite this publication as:
OECD (2020), *OECD Sovereign Borrowing Outlook 2020*, OECD Publishing, Paris, *https://doi.org/10.1787/dc0b6ada-en*.

ISBN 978-92-64-54344-7 (print)
ISBN 978-92-64-52921-2 (pdf)

OECD Sovereign Borrowing Outlook
ISSN 2306-0468 (print)
ISSN 2306-0476 (online)

Foreword

The 2020 edition of the *OECD Sovereign Borrowing Outlook*, with revised sections taking into account the impact of COVID-19 pandemic, provides data, information and background on sovereign borrowing needs and discusses funding strategies and debt management policies for the OECD area and country groupings, including:

- Central government gross borrowing requirements
- Central government marketable debt
- Developments in sovereign bond markets
- Sovereign issuance trends in emerging market and developing economies
- Governance of public debt in the times of global crisis

The information in this publication is primarily based on responses received to an annual survey on the borrowing needs of OECD governments circulated by the OECD's Bond Market and Public Debt Management Unit. This includes an update on trends and developments associated with sovereign borrowing requirements, funding strategies, market infrastructure and debt levels from the perspective of public debt managers. The *Outlook* makes a policy distinction between funding strategy and borrowing requirements. Central government marketable gross borrowing needs, or requirements, are calculated on the basis of budget deficits and redemptions. Funding strategy entails decisions on how borrowing needs are going to be financed using different instruments (e.g. long-term, short-term, nominal, indexed, etc.) and which distribution channels (auctions, tap, syndication, etc.) will be used.

Comments and questions should be addressed to the Bond Markets and Public Debt Management Unit within the Insurance, Private Pensions and Financial Markets Division of the OECD Directorate for Financial and Enterprise Affairs (e-mail: PublicDebt@oecd.org). Find out more about OECD work on bond markets and public debt management online at www.oecd.org/finance/public-debt/.

Acknowledgements

The *OECD Sovereign Borrowing Outlook* is part of the activities of the OECD Working Party on Public Debt Management, incorporated in the programme of work of the Directorate for Financial and Enterprise Affairs' Bond Markets and Public Debt Management Unit. This Borrowing Outlook was prepared by the OECD Bond Markets and Public Debt Management Unit (Fatos Koc (Head of the Unit) and Gary Mills (Statistician)). Carl M. Magnusson (Consultant) has provided statistical support on global sovereign bond markets and contributed to Chapter 2. OECD colleagues, Serdar Celik (Senior Policy Analyst), Alessandro Maravalle (Economist), Lukasz Rawdanowicz (Senior Economist) and Robert Patalano (Deputy Head of Division) have provided their valuable feedback to Chapter 1 and Chapter 2, and; Enes Sunel (Economist) and Martin Kessler (Economist) to Chapter 2. The following Steering Committee members Teppo Koivisto, (Chair; Treasury, Finland); Sir Robert Stheeman (The UK Debt Management Office); and Dr Tammo Tammo Diemer (Federal Republic of Germany Finance Agency) and Anthony Requin (Agence France Trésor) have provided their comments and suggestions to Chapter 1, and Cristina Casalinho (Portuguese Treasury and Debt Management Agency), Carol Brigham (Bank of Canada), Thorsten Meyer Larsen (Danmarks National Bank) have provided their valuable feedback to Chapter 3. Pamela Duffin (Communications Manager) and Edward Smiley (Publications Officer) have supported the whole team with invaluable publishing guidance and proof reading expertise.

Table of contents

FIGURES

Figures and data available at:
http://www.oecd.org/finance/public-debt/oecdsovereignborrowingoutlook.htm

TABLES

Follow OECD Publications on:

http://twitter.com/OECD_Pubs

http://www.facebook.com/OECDPublications

http://www.linkedin.com/groups/OECD-Publications-4645871

http://www.youtube.com/oecdilibrary

http://www.oecd.org/oecddirect/

Editorial

The COVID-19 pandemic is the most serious global health crisis in living memory. The virus and the policies put in place to slow its spread have precipitated a dramatic decline in economic activity, and OECD economies are now facing the worst recession since the Great Depression.

OECD governments have taken wide-ranging fiscal measures, complemented by central bank responses, to mitigate the shock. The rapid expansion of healthcare capacity and large-scale assistance programmes to households and businesses have been necessary to stave off the worst effects of the pandemic on both lives and livelihoods, but these responses have impacted public finances. Fiscal balances in OECD countries are projected to deteriorate by around 8% of GDP in 2020-21 on average.

This has given rise to steep increases in borrowing needs, and this edition of the annual *OECD Sovereign Borrowing Outlook* offers the first comprehensive picture of the immediate impact of Covid-19 on public borrowing needs since the pandemic began. The gross borrowing needs of OECD governments for 2020 have increased an estimated 30% compared to pre-COVID estimates, and outstanding central government debt is expected to increase from USD 47.1 trillion in 2019 to around USD 52.7 trillion by the end of 2020, USD 3.5 trillion higher than the pre-COVID estimate.

The increase in indebtedness and borrowing needs are considerable in their scale, and certainly much larger than during the Global Financial Crisis (GFC). The fiscal balance deterioration as a percentage of GDP during the pandemic is two-and-half-times greater than that seen at the height of the GFC in 2008-09. Central government marketable debt-to-GDP ratio for the OECD area, broadly unchanged since 2014, will increase by 13.4 % in 2020, compared with an increase of 8.7% of GDP in 2009.

Amidst these fiscal developments, central bank policy has been critical in alleviating immediate concerns over debt sustainability. Highly accommodative monetary policy has served to reduce borrowing costs, and a vast majority of bonds issued across the OECD in the first five months of 2020 were sold with interest rates below 1%. Further quantitative easing, following over a decade of asset purchase programmes, has made central banks the dominant holders of domestic government bonds in several key jurisdictions, while monetary policy was instrumental in calming markets and restoring confidence during a period of turmoil in March.

At the same time many emerging markets still face a challenging financing environment, and the *Outlook* provides novel insights about the impact of the COVID-19 pandemic on debt issuance conditions for these markets. Many emerging markets have increased issuance in local currency in recent years, which has helped address foreign exchange risk. However the pandemic has weighed considerably on investor sentiment and risk appetite to date, which has already translated to a sharp reversal of capital flows. Low income and non-investment grade issuers have been particularly hard hit.

Though monetary policy conditions are generally supportive across the OECD, any increase in today's financing needs implies higher debt repayments tomorrow. Given the surge in borrowings and resulting increase in debt redemptions, sovereign issuers must adapt borrowing operations to changing funding needs and investor demand, such as issuing new maturity lines or new types of securities, which can enable them to diversify funding resources.

At the time of publication a great deal of uncertainty remains about the course of the pandemic and its immediate and longer-term impacts. We do not know when the pandemic will end, or whether the worst of its social and economic costs are behind us. If conditions worsen governments may need to extend or create new assistance packages and may realise losses on state guarantees, which in turn will further deteriorate public finances. Sovereign issuance may increase even more from these already very high levels.

Sovereign debt offices have an important role to play in meeting the immediate financing needs of governments, in supporting well-functioning markets and in formulating long-term borrowing strategies during this crisis and beyond. This *Outlook* provides the data needed to monitor market developments and emerging risks, and provides an overview of practices and strategies across countries to best respond to recent developments and the times ahead.

Greg Medcraft

Director, OECD Directorate for Financial and Enterprise Affairs

Abbreviations and acronyms

ADB	Asian Development Bank
BCP	Business Continuity Plan
BoE	Bank of England
BOJ	Bank of Japan
CB	Central Bank
CBO	Congressional Budget Office
COVID	Coronavirus (COVID-19) disease
CUSIP	Committee on Uniform Security Identification Procedures
DMO	Debt Management Office
DSSI	Debt Service Suspension Initiative
ECB	European Central Bank
EFSM	European Financial Stabilisation Mechanism
EM	Emerging Market
ESM	European Stability Mechanism
EU	European Union
EUR	Euro
FILP	Fiscal Investment and Loan Program
FRNs	Floating Rate Notes
FX	Foreign Exchange
GBP	Great Britain Pound
GBR	Gross Borrowing Requirement
GDP	Gross Domestic Product
GFC	Global Financial Crisis
GFSR	Global Financial Stability Report
GNI	Gross National Income
ICE	Intercontinental Exchange
IFAWG	International Financial Architecture Working Group
IG	Investment Grade

10 |

IIF	Institute for International Finance
IMF	International Monetary Fund
ISIN	International Securities Identification Number
IT	Information Technology
LB	Liquidity Buffer
LCBM	Local Currency Bond Market
LICs	Low Income Countries
MENA	Middle East and North Africa
NBR	Net Borrowing Requirement
OECD	Organisation for Economic Co-operation and Development
PD	Primary Dealer
PEPP	Pandemic Emergency Purchase Programme
PSPP	Public Sector Purchase Programme
RIC	Reuters Instrument Code
SEK	Swedish Krona
SMEs	Small and Medium-sized Enterprises
SOFR	Secured Overnight Financing Rate
SURE	Support to mitigate Unemployment Risks in an Emergency
UK	United Kingdom
UNEDIC	Union Nationale Interprofessionnelle pour l'Emploi Dans l'Industrie et le Commerce
US	United States
USD	United States Dollar
WB	World Bank
WGBI	World Government Bond Index
WHO	World Health Organisation
WP	Working Paper
WPDM	Working Party on Debt management

Executive summary

Central government borrowings from the markets hit a record high in the first five months of 2020

The pandemic-related surge in government financing needs has resulted in OECD governments raising a record amount of funds from the market. From January to May 2020, governments issued debt securities worth USD 11 trillion – almost 70% higher than average issuance in the same period over the past five years. In addition to financing the COVID-19 rescue and related fiscal stimulus packages, increased precautionary financing and short-term cash needs to smooth out cash flow disruptions contributed to the surge in sovereign issuance during this period.

All OECD governments have revised up their borrowing estimates for the whole year, although to varying degrees depending on the extent to which they were hit by the pandemic, their fiscal capacity to address the shock and the types of fiscal measures implemented. A survey on the impact of the pandemic on the sovereign borrowing outlook among OECD sovereign debt management offices estimates that gross borrowing needs have increased by 30% compared to pre-COVID estimates to reach USD 28.8 trillion, about half of which is for short-term borrowing needs. While central government borrowing estimates have increased significantly in G7 economies, changes in OECD emerging-market economies have been rather limited.

Despite a temporary increase in March, borrowing costs have remained at very low levels, mainly owing to highly accommodative monetary policies. In the five months to end-May, about 25% of government bonds carried negative interest rates, and 43% of bond issuance was at interest rates between 0% and 1%. Compared to 2019, borrowing costs improved considerably in Canada, the United Kingdom and the United States.

Surging borrowing and tumbling GDP carry the debt-to-GDP ratio to an unprecedented level

For the OECD area as a whole, outstanding central government debt is expected to increase from USD 47 trillion in 2019 to USD 52.7 trillion at the end of 2020. At the same time, OECD economies, facing the deepest recession since the 1930s, are projected to contract by 7.5% in 2020, under a single-hit scenario which assumes a successful resolution of the current outbreak. The dramatic increase in borrowing needs and the decline in GDP mean that the central government marketable debt-to-GDP ratio for the OECD area is projected to increase by 13.4 percentage points to around 86% in 2020. For comparison purposes, this ratio rose by 12.6 percentage points between 2007 and 2009, during the global financial crisis.

Given the surge in borrowing needs, debt redemptions are set to increase substantially. OECD governments will need to refinance around 40% of their outstanding marketable debt in the next three years, notwithstanding that the majority of OECD countries experienced a sizeable elongation of debt maturity in the pre-COVID period, which has helped alleviate debt sustainability concerns in some countries. Another important factor that should be considered in refinancing risk assessments is low cost of sovereign borrowing and large-scale sovereign asset purchases by major central banks, which has facilitated funding of large government financing requirements.

While a strong fiscal response to support the recovery is essential and a one-off shock to the level of debt may not threaten debt sustainability if economies recover, controlling debt dynamics is also needed for achieving long-term debt sustainability. Looking forward, a failure to focus on ensuring debt sustainability once the recovery has accomplished would be an important source of risk, in particular for countries with weak debt dynamics.

Sovereign issuers have adapted borrowing operations to increasing funding needs and evolving market conditions

In the current environment, the key challenge for sovereign issuers is to increase issuance to finance policy responses, while avoiding a potential decline in market functioning. In response to this challenge, sovereign debt offices in several OECD countries have adjusted their borrowing operations with respect to issuance choice and techniques. While auctions are more frequent and larger, other issuance techniques such as syndications and private placements have also expanded since the pandemic.

More than two-thirds of OECD sovereign debt management offices have increased issuance of government securities across the yield curve, issuing more money market instruments such as T-Bills and repos compared to long-term bonds since the outbreak. Sovereign issuers typically view money market instruments as shock absorbers for any unexpected financing needs. For example, during the global financial crisis, several countries increased their T-Bill issuance temporarily, but moved towards longer-dated securities in the following years as market conditions improved and borrowing requirements remained elevated.

Increased budget deficits generate scope for issuance of new securities (e.g. Green bonds), or new longer-dated maturity lines. Introducing new instruments can contribute to enhancing the financing capacity of sovereigns, diversify their funding sources and mitigate medium and long-term refinancing risk. Such decisions require the careful consideration of several parameters, including investor needs, and the interest rate and maturity structure of existing debt.

Emergency cash management tools enable governments to meet extended obligations in times of global crisis

During the initial phase of the COVID-19 crisis, short-term funding needs of governments rose suddenly due to lower fiscal revenues to combat recession coupled with a massive jump in spending both on healthcare and stimulus. At the same time, widespread risk aversion in financial markets has hit funding conditions profoundly and rapidly. This situation posed significant challenges for government cash and debt managers, whose ultimate goal is to ensure that governments are able to meet their financial obligations in a timely manner.

The pandemic has underscored the importance of emergency funding mechanisms, such as cash buffers and credit lines for sovereign issuers in order to access liquidity as quickly as possible to manage unanticipated cash flows. The *Outlook* reveals that several debt offices in the OECD area have benefited from already available 'cash buffers' during these difficult times to finance government and avoid a temporary increase in borrowing costs in the market. In addition, having such measures in place has delivered positive signalling effects on market participants. Given the highly uncertain outlook, governments may also want to revise their cash buffer polices as a risk management tool to address potential challenges.

1. Sovereign borrowing outlook for OECD countries

Impact of the COVID-19 pandemic - To tackle the health crisis caused by the COVID-19 pandemic and its massive impact on economies and financial markets, governments and central banks of the OECD countries have deployed a wide range of measures since March 2020. In addition to large discretionary fiscal stimulus packages, automatic fiscal stabilisers have also led to sudden and significant increases in cash requirements. As a result, sovereign borrowing needs have surged in many countries.

During the first five months of this year, OECD governments increased their issuance of debt securities significantly, in total surpassing the historical average by almost 70% with significant variation across countries. The total market borrowing is expected to reach an unprecedented level of USD 28.8 trillion in bonds and bills in 2020. With interest rates are at record lows reducing the cost of borrowing in most OECD countries, the primary challenge for many sovereign issuers is to increase debt issuance significantly without undermining the functioning of sovereign bond markets.

1.1. Introduction

Chapter 1 of the 2020 OECD Sovereign Borrowing Outlook was published in February before the COVID-19 outbreak. The main objective of this second edition is to provide an overview of recent developments concerning government borrowing needs, funding conditions and funding strategies in the OECD area, and an update of the 2020 estimates released prior to the COVID-19 outbreak. The key source of information is a special survey of debt management offices of OECD countries on the impact of the crisis on public debt management.

In addition to an overview of sovereign debt developments in the OECD area, this chapter also discusses near and medium-term policy considerations for sovereign debt management in view of increased global uncertainties and higher government refinancing needs.

Key findings

- In the OECD area, the fiscal stimulus packages that have been introduced to mitigate the economic and social impact of the COVID-19 outbreak, leading to a sudden and dramatic increase in government borrowing needs. In addition, automatic fiscal stabilisers as well as the differences in time and size of cash flow estimates have led to rapid rises in cash needs in many countries.

- Despite generally volatile market conditions, OECD governments raised a record amount of funds from the markets during the first five months of 2020. The total amount of government securities issued between January and May 2020 reached USD 11 trillion, which was almost 70% higher than the average amount issued in the same period over the past five years.

- In the context of highly uncertain economic outlook for the rest of the year, the survey results indicate that gross borrowing needs of OECD governments will increase by almost 30% in 2020 compared with the pre-COVID estimates. Sovereign debt managers have reported that the current challenge is to increase issuance without undermining the functioning of sovereign debt markets.

- For the OECD area as a whole, outstanding central government debt is expected to increase from USD 47 trillion in 2019 to USD 52.7 trillion at the end of 2020. This is USD 3.5 trillion higher than the pre-COVID estimate. As a result of both the rapid increase in borrowing needs and the decline in GDP across OECD economies, the central government marketable debt-to-GDP ratio for the OECD area is projected to increase by 13.4 percentage points to around 86% in 2020, the largest increase in a single year since 2007.

- The sovereign debt management offices have taken steps to adapt their borrowing operations to a rapidly changing environment with respect to funding needs and investor demand. Main changes in borrowing operations have so far included an increase in the size and frequency of auctions; a larger use of syndications and other issuance techniques; a higher issuance of short-term financing instruments compared to long-term bonds; and the introduction of new maturity lines.

- As circumstances evolve, debt management offices continue to adjust their rules and practices. However, some of the measures taken are short-term in nature and will not fundamentally change the principles of debt management. It is therefore of a significant importance to communicate clearly with investors and other market participants the expected duration of new measures to avoid potential misinterpretations.

- The pandemic has underscored the importance of emergency funding tools for sovereign issuers in addressing short-term funding needs and avoiding a temporary increase in borrowing costs from the market. In the medium and long-term, preparedness for higher refinancing risk is critical for sovereign issuers with heavy debt repayment requirements. Policy makers should consider investor demand when adjusting their borrowing strategies to mitigate re-financing risk, and increase their financing capacity, such as by introducing new securities and diversifying the funding sources.

1.2. Surge in borrowing needs and outstanding debt

Across the OECD area, governments experienced sudden and dramatic increases in funding needs in the wake of the COVID-19 outbreak. Since mid-February, governments have stepped up their fiscal interventions (e.g. broad-based tax reliefs, wage subsidies, unemployment benefits, mortgage relief, lump-sum payments to households, loans and loan guarantees to businesses, as well as equity investments by governments in distressed companies) to weather the social and economic consequences of the pandemic (OECD, 2020[1]). During this period governments borrowing needs were revised upwards in most of the OECD countries as a result of the deterioration in the fiscal outlook posed by the COVID-19 outbreak. While upward revisions were largely driven by the second wave of fiscal measures by governments as the economic fallout from the pandemic proved more severe, changes in revenue streams also affected government cash needs.

Despite substantial fiscal policy support, global economic activity declined abruptly in the first quarter of 2020, and real GDP in the OECD area is projected to fall by 7.5% in 2020, provided that there is no second outbreak of the pandemic (OECD, 2020[1]). While large scale fiscal support programmes have been necessary to limit the economic and social damages of the pandemic, they have implications for the sovereign borrowing outlook. A combination of rising government borrowing requirements and collapsing economy is expected to propel debt-to-GDP ratios significantly higher.

1.2.1. Gross borrowings from the markets hit a record high level in the first five months of this year

OECD governments raised a record amount of funds from the market to finance the fiscal policy responses to the outbreak. The total amount of government securities issued during the first five months of 2020 reached USD 11 trillion. This was 69% higher than average issuance in the same period over the past five years. Most of the increased sovereign issuance across the OECD area aimed to finance the COVID-19 rescue and the related recovery packages. In addition, increased precautionary financing and short-term cash needs for smoothing out cash flow disruptions have also contributed to the surge in sovereign issuance by several countries during this period.

In the first two months of 2020, sovereign debt issuance in the OECD area was mostly in line with the historical averages. Following the spread of the outbreak across Europe and the United States which led to substantial fiscal policy support to cushion the economic blow, borrowing from the market started to accelerate towards the end of March and reached an unprecedented level in April. Although the total issuance decreased from USD 3.8 trillion in April to USD 2 trillion in May, this was still more than double the average amount of securities issued in the same month during the past five years (Figure 1.1, Panel A). The increase in issuance amounts was mainly driven by the United States (Figure 1.1, Panel B), where issuance was already higher than the historical average prior to the pandemic shock. Issuance by the euro area governments, which was lower than the historical averages in January and February, also increased sharply in April. Also, several sovereign issuers including Canada, Germany and the United Kingdom doubled their issuance amounts compared to the average over the same period of the past five years.

Figure 1.1. Sovereign debt issuance between January and May 2020, USD trillion

Panel A: Comparison of debt securities issued in 2020 and the previous 5 years' averages

Panel B: Issuer composition in total issuance between Jan-May 2020

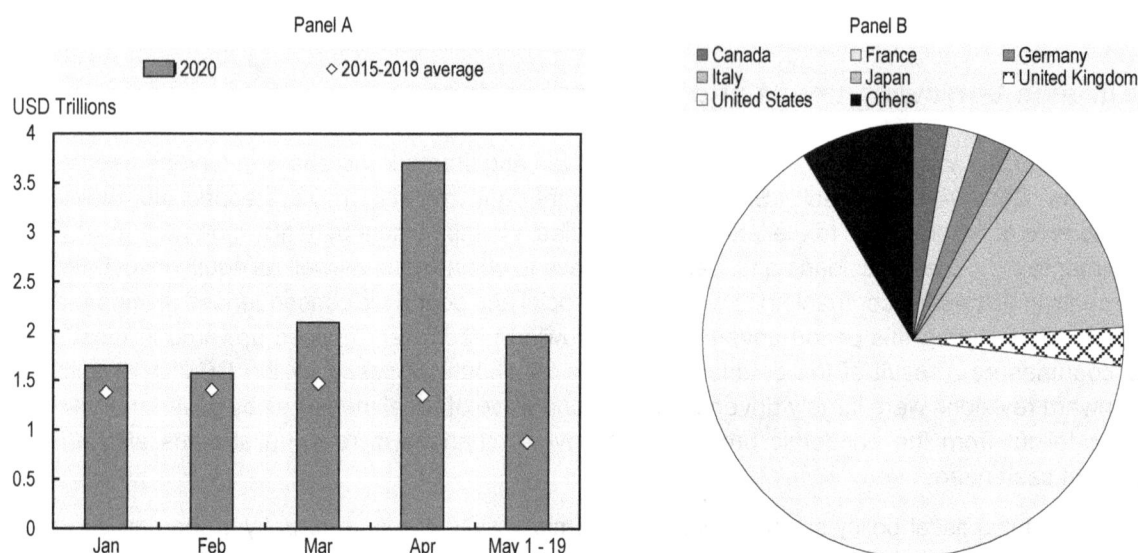

Notes: Both charts are based on data consisting of new issues and re-opens. Panel A: Where applicable currency conversions were calculated on the day of issuance or re-open
Source: Refinitiv; OECD calculations.

1.2.2. The surge in annual borrowing needs results in fast pace debt accumulation

The recent survey on the impact of the pandemic on sovereign borrowing outlook reveals that gross borrowing needs of OECD governments for 2020 have increased by 30% compared to pre-COVID estimates (Table 1.1). Amid the exceptionally uncertain economic outlook, sovereign issuance might further increase, depending on the pace of economic recovery and need for additional stimulus packages.

Total annual issuance of government securities is expected to increase by USD 6.5 trillion to USD 28.8 trillion as of the end of 2020. It is important to note that the uncertainty in the economic conditions makes it difficult to estimate the amount of short-term debt that will be rolled-over by the end of 2020. Therefore, the 2020 estimates consider that the proportion of short and long-term debt issuances and redemptions will remain in line with the pre-COVID averages. Based on this assumption, the standardised gross borrowing requirements, excluding short-term borrowing to fund horizons of less than one year, point to a rise of USD 3.5 trillion to USD 15.4 trillion.[1] As a result, the outstanding central government marketable debt is expected to increase by 7.2% and reach USD 52.7 trillion at the end of 2020. It should be noted that there are considerable risks that the sovereign borrowing will be higher than currently expected.

The survey results revealed that all OECD governments have revised up their borrowing estimates for 2020 in the wake of the COVID-19 crisis, but to a varying degree mainly depending on the extent to which they were hit by the pandemic and their fiscal capacity to address the shock. While central government borrowing estimates have increased significantly in most advanced economies, changes in OECD emerging-market economies have been rather limited. In the United States, for example, the Congressional Budget Office (CBO) projects a USD 3.7 trillion deficit in 2020, which is nearly three time larger than the prior estimate. As a result of the expected large increase in the budget deficit, the US accounts for the bulk of the additional post-Covid borrowing needs in the OECD area. Both the significant rise in the US budget deficit due to the policy responses to the pandemic and the expected size of the cash balance have led to a large and rapid increase in net supply of government securities (US Treasury, May 5, 2020[2]). In total, the US Treasury expects borrowing needs to amount to USD 4.5 trillion in 2020 based on estimates in May. Contrary to the recent years when the government's borrowing needs were quite stable, Germany has also seen a rapid surge in gross borrowing needs since March (German Finanzagentur, 2020[3]).[2] In addition, the annual borrowing needs have increased significantly in Canada, and the United Kingdom.

Estimated borrowing needs and debt stock in 2020, OECD (as of May 2020)

Table 1.1. Central government gross borrowing needs and outstanding debt for 2020

OECD	pre-COVID, trillions USD	post-COVID, trillions USD
Gross Borrowing	22.2	28.8
Standardised Gross Borrowing	11.8	15.4
Debt stock	49.1	52.7

Note: Central government marketable definition is used for government borrowing and debt estimates. Standardised Gross Borrowing subtracts the value of short-term redemptions in 2020 (i.e. within short-term borrowing it is the net issuance). For post-COVID estimates it is assumed that over the full year the proportion of short and long-term debt issuances and redemptions are the same as in the pre-COVID period.
Source: 2019 Survey on Central Government Marketable Debt and Borrowing; 2020 Survey on the impact of the pandemic on public debt management; *OECD Economic Outlook, https://doi.org/10.1787/0d1d1e2e-en*; Refinitiv; national authorities' websites; and OECD calculations.

Figure 1.2. Post-COVID increase in nominal debt stock.

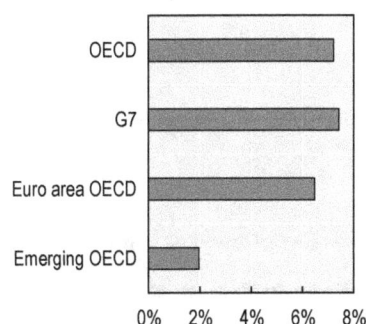

Note: Central government marketable definition is used for government borrowing and debt estimates. For post-COVID estimates it is assumed that over the full year the proportion of short and long-term debt issuances and redemptions are the same as in the pre-COVID period.
Source: 2019 Survey on Central Government Marketable Debt and Borrowing; 2020 Survey on the impact of the pandemic on public debt management; *OECD Economic Outlook, https://doi.org/10.1787/0d1d1e2e-en*; Refinitiv; national authorities' websites; and OECD calculations

In some other advanced OECD economies, such as France and Ireland, changes in annual central government borrowing needs have – so far – been relatively limited. This can be explained to some extent by the differences in the design and implementation of fiscal measures. For example, some forms of fiscal measures taken against the pandemic, such as provision of government guarantees, have no direct impact on public finances. In some cases also a large portion of the social security benefits have been financed through existing social safety nets and automatic insurance mechanisms without a need for significant additional central governments funding (e.g. France).[3] In some cases, governments have also used other available resources such as wealth funds and contingency funds to finance fiscal measures (e.g. Chile, Ireland and Switzerland).

1.2.3. The combined effect of the increase in expenditure and the fall in GDP grounds an unprecedented jump in the debt to GDP ratio

Based on current budget projections, gross borrowing requirements as a percentage of GDP are expected to increase from around 33% in 2019 to 47% in 2020 (Figure 1.3. Panel A). This 14 percentage point jump in gross borrowing requirements to GDP ratio exceeds the rise that occurred between 2008 and 2009 during the global financial crisis (GFC).

As shown in Table 1.1 above, outstanding central government debt for the OECD area as a whole is expected to increase from USD 47 trillion in 2019 to USD 52.7 trillion at the end of 2020. As a result of the surge in outstanding debt and the contraction in economies, the survey estimates that the central government marketable debt-to-GDP ratio for the OECD area, broadly unchanged since 2014, will increase from 72.8%in 2019 to 86.2% in 2020 (Figure 1.3. Panel B). Since fiscal policy is expected to remain supportive across OECD economies, in particular for domestic demand, and some of the measures put in place have medium-term financing implications, central government debt is likely to remain high. It should be noted that the scope of the survey is limited to central governments, and given the widespread coverage of fiscal packages introduced by some OECD countries in response to the COVID-19 crisis, the rise in public debt might be higher than that in central government debt.[4]

Figure 1.3. Central government marketable gross borrowing and debt in OECD countries, 2007-2020, as a percentage of GDP

Panel A: Gross borrowing as a percentage of GDP, Panel B: Debt stock as a percentage of GDP

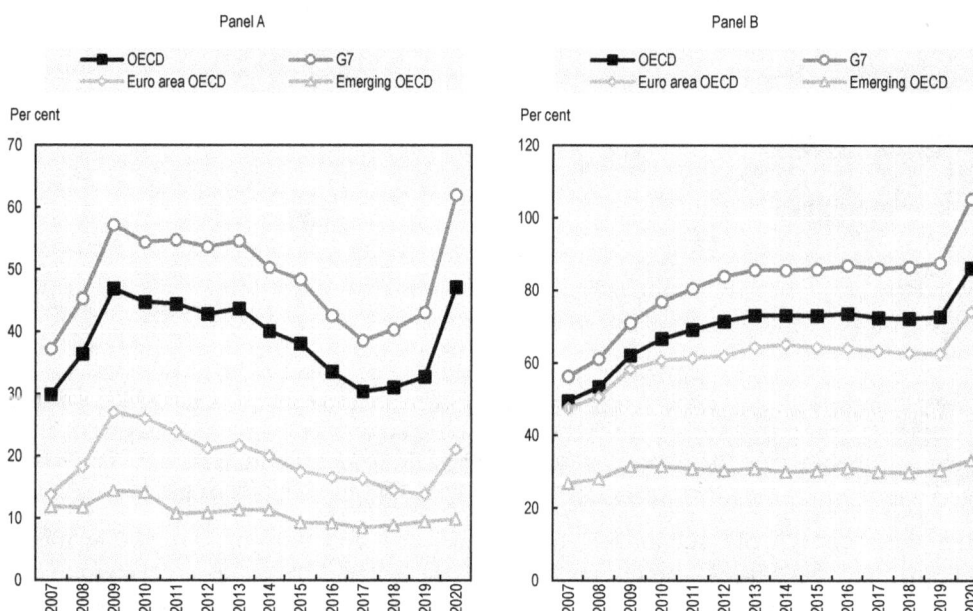

Note: Central government marketable debt
Source: 2019 Survey on Central Government Marketable Debt and Borrowing; 2020 Survey on the impact of the pandemic on public debt management; *OECD Economic Outlook, https://doi.org/10.1787/0d1d1e2e-en*; Refinitiv; national authorities' websites; and author calculations.

Total outstanding debt to GDP ratios are influenced by a combination of factors, including economic growth rates, governments' borrowing needs. Panel B of Figure 1.3 illustrates three periods of change in total central government debt stock of OECD countries since 2007. The first one is the GFC period, when the central government debt-to-GDP ratios were lifted to a higher level as a result of the increased borrowing needs. Between 2007 and 2009, the central government debt-to-GDP ratio for the OECD area increased by 12.6 percentage points. In the second period from 2010 to 2013, the debt-to-GDP ratio for the OECD area increased by 11 percentage points mainly reflecting the euro area debt crisis. During the last period that started in 2014 and continued until the end of 2019, the ratio was broadly unchanged at around 70%. This was largely due to favourable interest rate-growth differentials in most OECD countries. After this fairly stable period, the debt-to-GDP level is expected to increase by 13.4 percentage points from 2019 to 2020 due to the impact of the pandemic on government spending and revenues. This is the largest rise in a single year since 2007.

The impact of the pandemic on government indebtedness differs widely among OECD countries depending on the social and economic impact of the crisis and the governments' fiscal capacity to address the shock. As a percentage of GDP, the increases in both the gross borrowing needs and debt ratios of G7 and euro area countries are expected to be significant, while those of OECD emerging-market economies are relatively small. At the same time, supported by central banks' government bond purchase programmes and short term interest rate set close to the zero lower bound, has contributed to flatten the sovereign bond yield curve across all maturities. Issuance of long-term debt at very low interest rates has helped alleviate debt sustainability concerns, particularly in major advanced economies.

The OECD Economic Outlook of June 2020 concluded that a one-off shock to the level of debt may not on its own endanger debt sustainability if economies recover. Nevertheless a lack of focus on ensuring debt sustainability once the recovery has firmed would be an important risk (OECD, 2020[11]). In the euro area, in addition to the national fiscal support, EU and euro area bodies have introduced several initiatives to help member states, especially those hard-hit by the pandemic and with less fiscal space, some of which would have no implications for national debt burdens.[5]

1.3. Adapting borrowing operations to rapidly changing circumstances

In response to the dramatic and sudden increases in borrowing needs and changing market conditions, sovereign debt management offices (DMOs) in several OECD countries have adjusted their borrowing strategies. Table 1.2 summaries the survey results with respect to the adaption of instrument choice, the auction specifics and the use of other issuance techniques in the new market environment.

Table 1.2. Survey results concerning the changes in borrowing operations

	In the last 4 months	For 2020 overall
Instruments		
Issuance of securities across the yield curve	24 higher, 3 lower, 6 no change	29 higher, 1 lower, 3 no change
Issuance of money market instruments (i.e. T-Bills and repos) compared to issuance of long-term bonds	26 higher, 1 lower, 5 no change	23 higher, 4 lower, 5 no change
Introducing new maturity lines	17 yes, 15 no	21 yes, 10 no
Issuing new types of securities (e.g. FRNs, Green bonds, Linkers)	0 yes, 31 no	2 yes, 24 no
Auctions		
Changes in auction calendar	22 yes, 11 no	23 yes, 10 no
Frequency of auctions	19 higher, 0 lower, 14 no change	21 higher, 0 lower, 12 no change
Post-auction option facility (non-competitive bids)	4 higher, 2 lower, 27 no change	5 higher, 2 lower, 26 no change
Other issuance techniques		
Use of syndications	12 higher, 1 lower, 20 no change	15 higher, 0 lower, 18 no change
Use of private placements	7 higher, 0 lower, 26 no change	6 higher, 0 lower, 27 no change

Source: 2020 Survey on the impact of the pandemic on public debt management.

More than two-thirds of OECD DMOs indicated an increased issuance of government securities across the yield curve, and a higher use of money market instruments compared to long-term bonds since the outbreak.[6] Furthermore, they introduced (or are planning to introduce) new maturity lines during the rest of the year. For example, German DMO (*Finanzagentur*) is adding 7- and 15- year maturity bonds to its new borrowing programme. Similarly, France and the United States launched a new 20- year bond in May, which appeals to investors looking for longer-duration securities such as pension funds and insurance companies.[7]

As discussed in the previous editions of this publication, sovereign issuers typically view money market instruments as shock-absorbers for any unexpected financing needs. Frequently, short-term financing is replaced by long-term instruments in the period following the shock. For example, during the GFC, several countries including France, Germany, the Netherlands and the United States, increased their T-Bill issuance temporarily. Consequently, more than 55% of the total funding requirement of OECD governments was raised through T-Bills in 2008. In the following years, while borrowing requirements remained elevated, maturity choices of most OECD countries have leaned towards long-dated securities in order to mitigate roll-over risk. The recent survey results indicate that DMOs are adapting a similar strategy in response to the pandemic shock.

Reflecting the changes in borrowing operations, the majority of the DMOs reported adjustments in quarterly and annual auction calendars. Most of the adjustments involve the size and frequency of auctions, as well as instrument choices. Other changes include a post-auction option facility.[8] For example, the UK DMO (which introduced a post-auction option facility in 2009) increased the additional amount that successful bidders can purchase through the facility from 10% to 25% of the nominal amount allocated as of April 2020 (The UK DMO, 2020[4]).

In terms of other issuance techniques, the use of syndications and private placements has expanded among the OECD DMOs since the outbreak. A number of countries including Australia, Austria, Germany, Ireland and the United Kingdom have reported a wider use of syndications, which are particularly used for inaugural issuance as an attempt to mitigate potential difficulties that investors face during the price discovery process. Some countries including Finland, Israel and Poland find it useful to supplement their regular auctions with private placements in an attempt to meet different investor preferences. Private placements, in general, are designed to meet the needs of a specific group of investors and enable issuers to raise funds through a private sale of securities to a limited number of qualified investors without a prior announcement.

Several sovereign debt managers noted that a key driving factor for funding strategies will be the change in investors' demand for a range of instruments with different maturity and interest-rate characteristics. In addition, they emphasised that the pandemic has required them to adapt borrowing operations to rapidly changing circumstances, but it has not fundamentally changed their approach to debt management. In this regard, they stressed that the temporary nature of some modifications should be communicated clearly with investors to avoid potential misinterpretations. It was also highlighted that the uncertainty around the epidemiological outlook - along with its potential impact on the economies and investor confidence - have an important bearing on the future course of government measures and the resilience of the financial sector.

1.4. Funding conditions have improved, but are still fragile

1.4.1. The turmoil in March

Sovereign debt managers of OECD countries reported that risk aversion in financial markets rose substantially at the beginning of the COVID-19 outbreak, and as investors' preference shifted towards cash (and cash-like instruments), selling pressure put strains on primary dealers' balance sheets. A few countries also highlighted the impact of widespread remote working practices in financial markets, which slowed dealer quotes and trades and contributed to low liquidity and relatively high volatility in the second half of March. The volatility manifested itself in various secondary market indicators including spikes in yields, maturity spreads, and bid- ask spreads in cash and derivative markets. While liquidity conditions in both on-the-run and off-the-run securities have deteriorated, off-the-run securities in particular were affected more strongly.

Figure 1.4. Evolution of yields on 10- year benchmark government bonds, G7

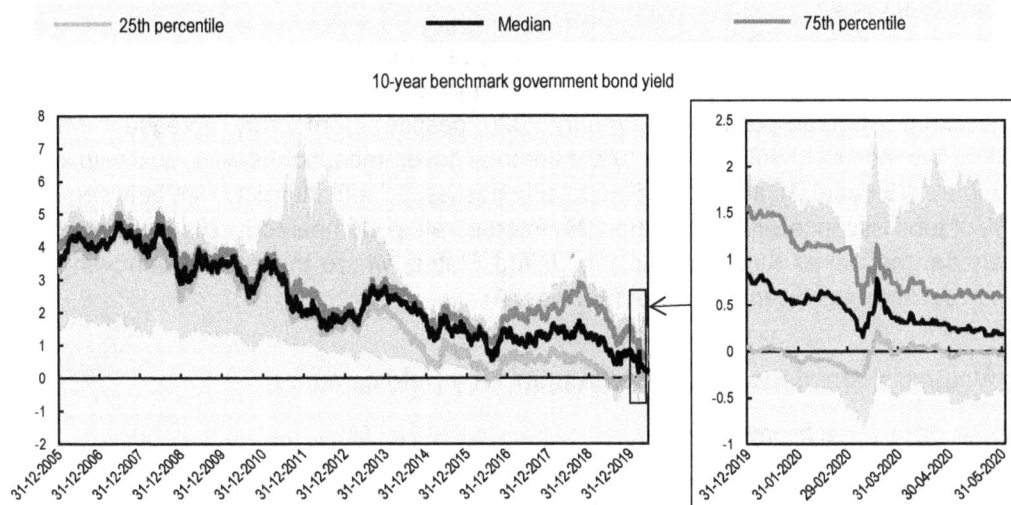

Note: Interest rates in percentages. Charts show the evolution of several metrics (grey area is difference between minimum and maximum, 25th percentile, 75th percentile, median) of 10 year benchmark government bond yields, calculated for G7 countries.
Source: Refinitiv; OECD calculations.

Following announcements by major central banks, in particular the Federal Reserve and the ECB, that they would support financial markets, including via buying large amounts of debt securities, stress in financial markets eased (Figure 1.4). However, market conditions have remained relatively challenging in a few countries, especially those hard-hit by the pandemic and with less fiscal leeway (e.g. Italy and Spain) (Figure 1.5).

Figure 1.5. 10- and 2- year benchmark government bond yields in Italy and Spain

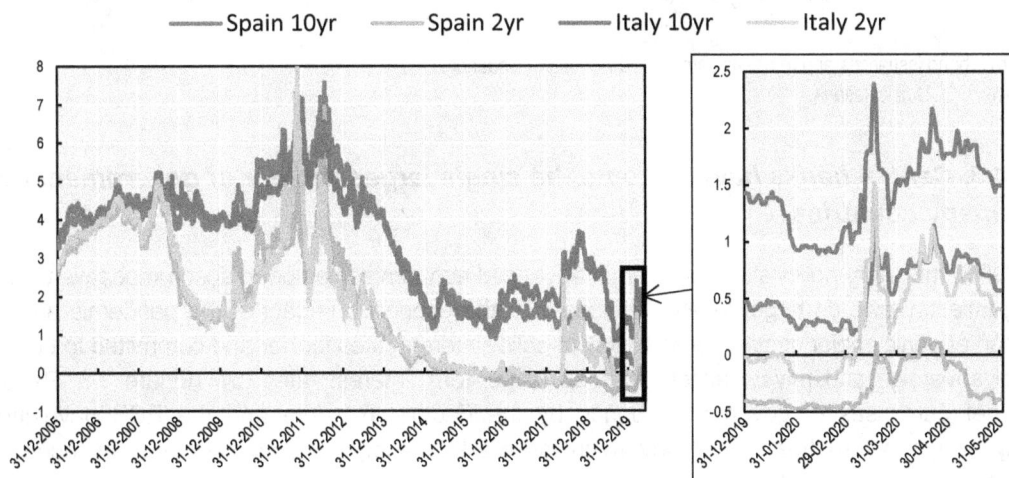

Note: Interest rates in percentages.
Source: Refinitiv; OECD calculations.

1.4.2. Interest rates on government debt remained at record lows

After the initial shock in March, interest rates on government debt returned to pre-crisis levels in many countries, reducing financing pressures on sovereign issuers, and helping them facilitate debt service. Low interest rates reflect a confluence of factors including stronger demand for safe assets and more accommodative monetary policies in most major advanced and emerging-market economies. They help lower debt servicing costs.

Despite the surge in debt issuance, government yield curves in many countries have shifted down in recent months. For example, average 10-year government bond yields in large advanced economies have fallen by more than 0.5 percentage point since January 2020, despite a temporary increase in March (Figure 1.4). In the first five months of 2020, about 70%of the total government bonds were sold with interest rates below 1% (Figure 1.6 Panel B), and 27% of the total bonds issued with interest rates between 1% and 2%, and only 5% of total issuance with higher than 2% interest rates. Compared to 2019, major changes took place in Canada, the United Kingdom and the United States, where the cost of borrowing across the maturities has declined significantly (Figure 1.6 Panel A).

Figure 1.6. Volume share of fixed-rate bond issuance by yield category

Panel A: full year 2019; Panel B: 2020 Jan-May

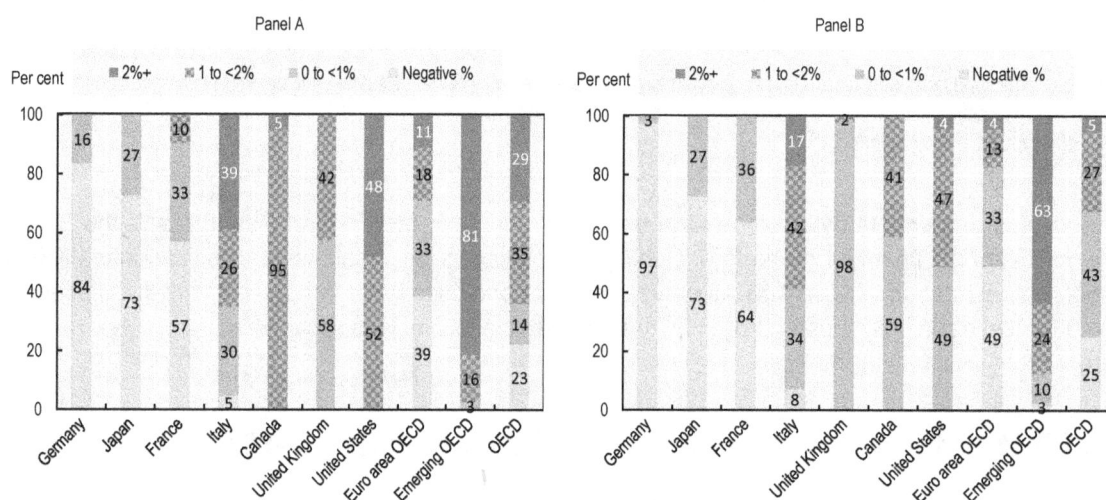

Notes: Fixed-rate bond issuances and re-opens categorised by yield at issuance.
Source: Refinitiv; OECD calculations.

1.4.3. Central banks have become the single largest holder of government bonds in many countries

Since the GFC, monetary policy stances in major advanced economies has been accommodative with the aim of bringing inflation towards target levels. To cope with the economic impact of the pandemic and ensuing financial market panic, major central banks have cut policy interest rates further and committed to buying large amounts of sovereign and private assets to keep longer-term interest rates low (Figure 1.8, Panel B). In particular, net purchases of government bonds by the Federal Reserve and the ECB have increased significantly, which in turn has helped sovereign issuers to manage funding pressures in recent months (Figure 1. 7).

Figure 1.7. Net purchases of government securities by major central banks (monthly), millions USD

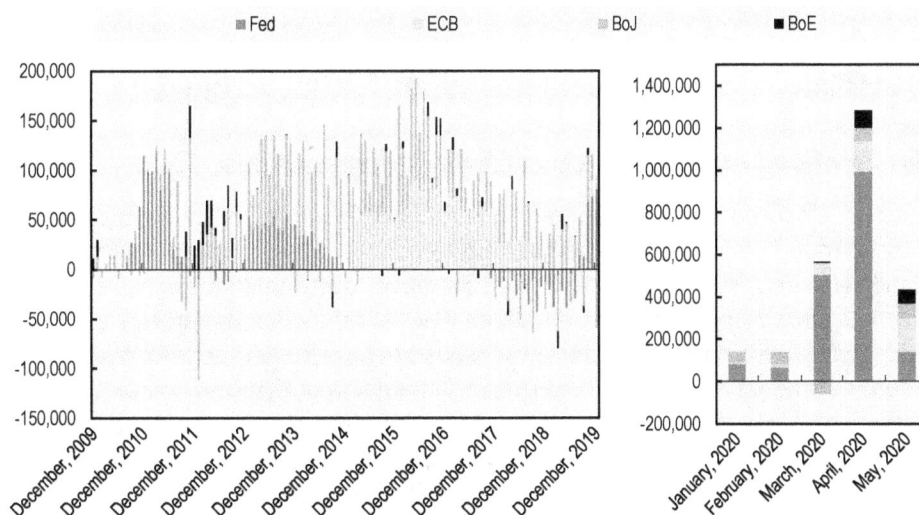

Note: Converted into USD at the end of each month. Calculated from data on security holdings for the Federal Reserve and the BoJ. For the BoE these data are calculated from holdings of gilts by the Bank of England's asset purchase facility. Data for ECB are net purchases for the PSPP and the PEPP.
Source: Central banks.

Figure 1.8.Several central banks have become dominant holders of domestic government bonds

Panel A: Central bank holdings of domestic government bonds as a % of total outstanding marketable bonds.
Panel B: Change in policy interest rates since end-2019 and 4 June 2020.

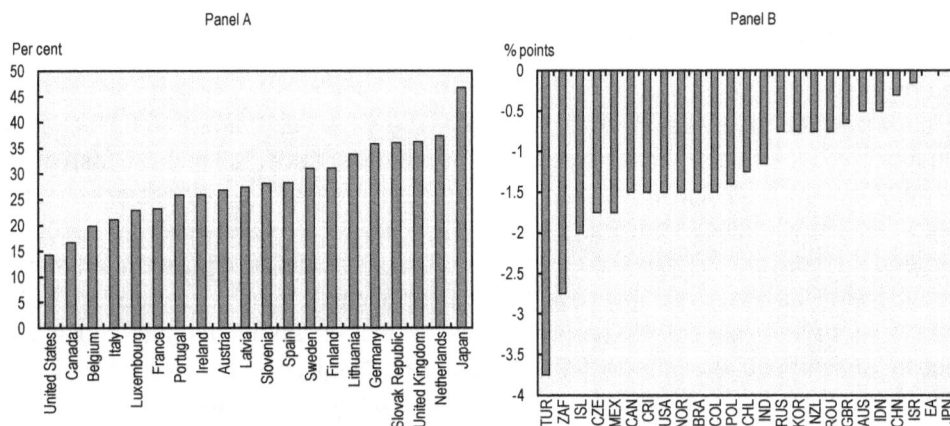

Note: See Annex 1.A.
Source: Panel A: OECD Economic Outlook 107 database; Board of Governors of the Federal Reserve System; US Department of the Treasury, Bureau of Fiscal Services; Bank of Canada; Bank of Japan; Ministry of Finance Japan; Sveriges Riksbank; Swedish central government debt statistics; UK Debt Management Office; Bank of England; European Central Bank; and OECD calculations. Panel B: OECD Economic Outlook 107 database; Refinitiv; and OECD calculations.

Large-scale asset purchases by central banks since the GFC have significantly changed the investor base for sovereign debt. This trend has accelerated with increasing net purchases in recent months and further strengthened the position of central banks as the single largest investor in sovereign debt in several OECD economies. Importantly, this trend has also been coupled with a marked increase in outstanding government debt in recent years. For instance, the central bank holds more than 45% of national government debt in Japan, around 30% in Germany, the Netherlands and the United Kingdom and above 20% in France, Ireland and Austria (Figure 1.8).

1.5. Near and medium-term policy considerations for sovereign debt management

1.5.1. Greater need for emergency cash management tools

The pandemic has underscored the importance of emergency funding tools for sovereign DMOs. While large uncertainties surrounding the outlook persist (e.g. a second wave of the pandemic or lower-than-expected economic recovery), market volatility might increase, governments might need to extend the scope and duration of support programmes, introduce new fiscal packages later in 2020. Against this background, having access to emergency funding tools has become more crucial for flexibility in issuance plans (e.g. uncovered auctions) and to avoid interruption in funding government expenses. If not already available, sovereign issuers, in particular the ones with heavy debt repayments in the near term might benefit from establishing an emerging funding mechanism, such as emergency cash buffers, credit lines with commercial banks and a short-term cash advance facility from the central bank.

Cash buffers have proven to be effective in addressing short-term funding needs and avoiding a temporary increase in borrowing costs from the market. The survey reveals that a few DMOs, noting the benefit of keeping a cash buffer in times of turmoil in March, have increased the size of cash buffers (e.g. Canada, Portugal and the United States). For example, the US Treasury is planning to increase the expected cash balance to USD 800 billion by the end of September. The desire to run a higher cash balance over the next few quarters reflects prudent risk management, given the larger size and greater uncertainty of cash outflows. Another example of contingency option for managing cash flows came from the United Kingdom, where the Bank of England has temporarily extended the use of the government's 'Ways and Means (W&M) facility' to manage liquidity and the short-term volatility of cash forecasts.

1.5.2. Preparedness for higher refinancing risk

The projected high level of new borrowing needs in 2020, in combination with amounts to be refinanced, will increase future debt repayments and might exacerbate pre-crisis public finance challenges with respect to heavy refinancing requirements. While some of the fiscal measures entail one-off cash transfers, most of them have medium-term financing implications. Even though monetary policy has been accommodative and low interest rates have reduced government debt servicing costs, substantial debt accumulation has resulted in larger debt repayments.[9] The increased central banks holdings of government marketable debt play an important role in the assessment of sovereign refinancing risk. If they continue to roll over the stock of public debt in their balance sheets, the refinancing risk would remain unchanged. Looking forward, the economic recovery might require additional fiscal support resulting in a further increase in sovereign debt stock. Against this background, preparedness for higher refinancing risk in the medium and long-term, is of critical importance for sovereign issuers facing heavy debt repayments.

An important development in recent months has been the shortening of average maturity of borrowing in the OECD area. The objective of sovereign debt management is often defined as "to ensure that the government's financing needs and its payment obligations are met at the lowest possible cost over the medium- to long-run, consistent with a prudent degree of risk". In order to achieve this goal, sovereign issuers set funding strategies in a way that strikes a balance between minimising interest expenses and refinancing risks, considering market conditions. In times of crisis, sovereign issuers prioritise ensuring funding without deteriorating the functioning of government securities markets over refinancing risk concerns. While short-term securities cost less than long-term securities –in a positive (normal) yield curve environment- they must be rolled over in short periods, which in turn increases issuers' exposure to market developments. This policy, while is effective in short-term, would lead higher roll-over ratios if it continues for longer periods.

As discussed in the previous section, sovereign issuers in many OECD countries have expanded their short-term borrowing programmes to manage unexpected surges in financing needs following the COVID-19 outbreak. The share of short-term instruments in total issuance by OECD governments in the first 20 weeks of 2020 is 73%. Even though this amount includes short-term borrowing needs that will unlikely be rolled-over, it is quite high compared with historical figures (Figure 1.9). In order to reduce rollover risks, maturity choices could lean towards longer-dated securities, taking into account the trade-off between expected cost and risk of short and long-term borrowing choices.

Figure 1.9. Maturity composition of central government marketable debt issuance

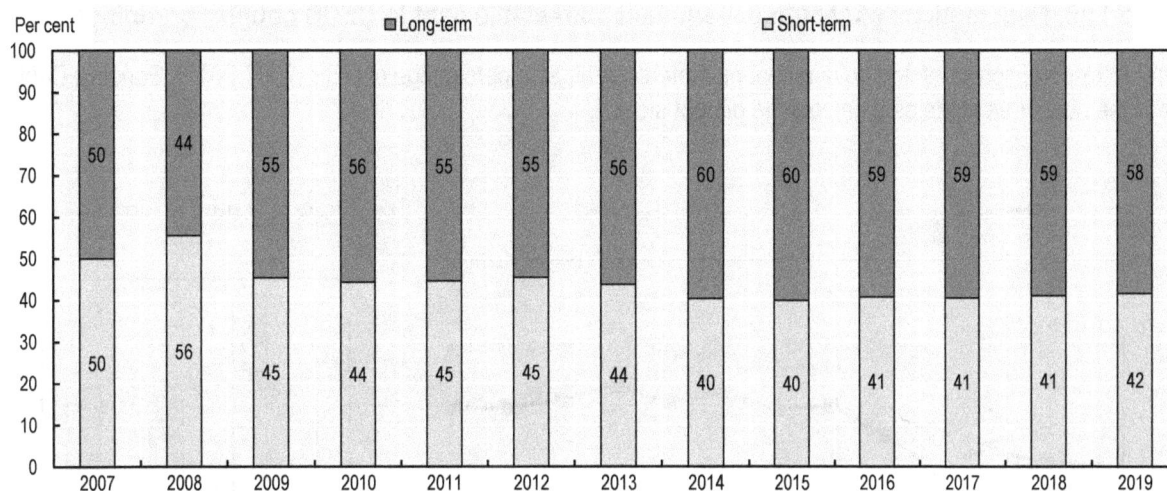

Notes: These are based on standardised gross borrowing figures.
Source: Data between 2007 and 2019 are from the 2019 Survey on Central Government Marketable Debt and Borrowing; *OECD Economic Outlook*, https://doi.org/10.1787/0d1d1e2e-en; Refinitiv; national authorities' websites; and OECD calculations.

In the OECD area, the medium and long-term debt redemption profile increased dramatically in the post-GFC period, but has stabilised around 7.5% of GDP in recent years (Figure 1.10, Panel A). In the next three years, governments will need to refinance around 40% of their outstanding marketable debt (Figure 1.10, Panel B). Given the surge in borrowing needs in response to the pandemic, redemptions will also further increase. This call for vigilance for sovereign issuers, in particular in the countries where increasing new funding requirements coincides with heavy repayments, on the global risks in the coming periods.

In countries where the increase in borrowing requirements has been substantial, sovereign issuers may benefit from increasing their financing capacity by introducing new securities, or adjusting existing products. Introducing new securities with long-term maturities, in particular, would not only help mitigate refinancing risks in the medium and long-term, but also generate additional demand from available domestic and international savings pools. Also, the diversification of funding sources reduces the reliance on any one group of investors.

In deciding on a new maturity line, or a new security type, a critical issue to assess is the presence of strong and sustainable investor demand for such debt. From the debt managers' perspective, it can be extremely difficult and costly to develop a market for a new instrument and also continue to implement a predictable government financing programme in the absence of a robust and viable investor demand (OECD, 2018[5]). In addition, sovereign issuers should consider the potential "cannibalisation" of liquidity in existing bonds with similar maturities.[10] When a large group of investors shifts from an existing maturity segment to a new one, this development can undermine market liquidity for the existing segment. However, when borrowing needs increase substantially and are expected to remain so in medium to long-term, it is possible to issue new instruments without harming the liquidity of existing ones with similar characteristics.

Increased budget deficits may further encourage some sovereigns, who had planned to issue new instruments prior to the COVID-19 outbreak, to increase the volume of such issuance. For example, a few sovereign issuers including Denmark, Germany and Sweden, have announced their plans to issue debut green bonds in 2020. Similarly, the US Treasury decided to introduce the secured overnight financing rate (SOFR)-linked bond in 2019. Inaugural issuances of such new instruments might offer higher volumes as total funding needs have risen substantially. It should be noted that providing adequate supply of new securities can help to enhance secondary market liquidity, and thereby lower liquidity premia and cost of borrowing.

Figure 1.10. Redemptions of central government marketable debt in OECD country groupings

Panel A: Redemption of central government marketable debt, as a percentage of GDP (2007-2019), Panel B: Debt due in the next three years as a percentage of debt stock

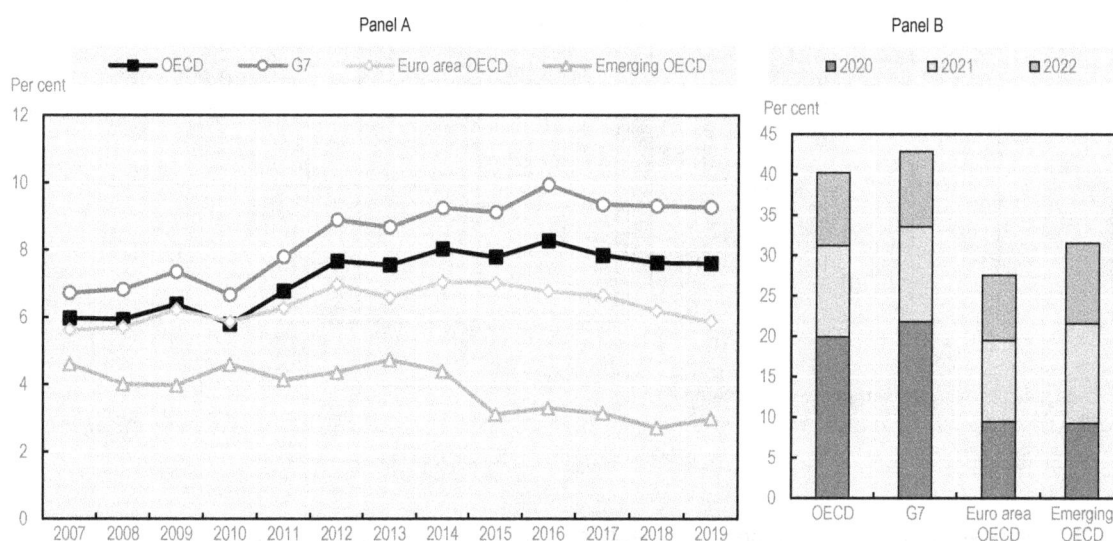

Notes: Panel A is medium and long-term redemptions as a percentage of GDP, Panel B also includes short-term debt with data as of 8 June 2020.
Source: Panel A, 2019 Survey on Central Government Marketable Debt and Borrowing; *OECD Economic Outlook*, https://doi.org/10.1787/0d1d1e2e-en; Refinitiv; national authorities' websites; and OECD calculations. Panel B, Refinitiv

1.5.3. Reviewing and adapting business continuity plans for pandemics

Similar to other businesses, the COVID-19 pandemic affects business operations of sovereign DMOs in terms of health and safety of workers, while the fiscal response to the pandemic weighed on funding needs in most OECD countries. Against this background, ensuring the continuity of the funding and cash management activities of DMOs has become critical for the continuity of governments' fight against the pandemic.

As discussed in detail in Chapter 3, many DMOs have activated their business continuity plans (BCPs) at early stages of the outbreak to ensure that their critical functions (government financing and debt repayments) are resilient during the crisis. Most DMOs have been carrying out operations including auctions, payments and transactions, and cash management partly or completely remotely since end-March. Also, split operations have been conducted to limit the risk of contagion. OECD DMOs reported that teleworking has functioned unexpectedly well, albeit some initial challenges (e.g. lack of technical equipment).

Looking forward, identification of gaps in business continuity plans would help to improve preparedness for potential future virus outbreaks (e.g. a second wave of COVID-19). Once the crisis is over or has subsided, sovereign DMOs should review their business continuity and recovery plans in light of the lessons learned during the COVID-19 pandemic. Identification of gaps in BCPs or necessary equipment to be acquired would help to improve their preparedness for potential future virus outbreaks. Furthermore, the use and priority of secondary sites might be worth reviewing as the recent experience of wide-scale remote working experience has proved to be effective in managing certain type of stress scenarios.

References

German Finanzagentur (2020), "Issues planned by the Federal government in the second quarter of 2020", *Press release*, Vol. April, https://www.deutsche-finanzagentur.de/fileadmin/user_upload/pressemeldungen/en/2020/2020-03-23_pm01_EK_Q2_en.pdf. [3]

OECD (2020), *OECD Economic Outlook, Volume 2020 Issue 1*, OECD Publishing, Paris, https://dx.doi.org/10.1787/0d1d1e2e-en. [1]

OECD (2018), "Sovereign Borrowing Outlook", OECD Publishing, Paris, https://doi.org/10.1787/23060476. [5]

OECD (2014), *OECD Sovereign Borrowing Outlook 2014*, OECD Publishing, Paris, https://dx.doi.org/10.1787/sov_b_outlk-2014-en. [6]

The UK DMO (2020), "Official Operations in the Gilt Market", *Operational Notice*, https://www.dmo.gov.uk/media/16394/opnot060420.pdf. [4]

US Treasury (May 5, 2020), "Minutes of the Meeting of the Treasury Borrowing Advisory Committee of the Securities Industry and Financial Markets Association", https://home.treasury.gov/news/press-releases/sm1003. [2]

Annex 1.A. Methods and sources

Definitions

- *Standardised Gross borrowing requirement* (GBR) for a year is equal to net borrowing requirement during that year plus the redemptions on the capital market at the beginning of the same year. Also, the (estimated) cash balance may affect the funding needs. In other words, the size of GBR in calendar year amounts to how much the DMO needs to issue in nominal terms so as to fully pay back maturing debt plus the net cash borrowing requirement through any issuance mechanism.

- *Net* borrowing *requirement (NBR)* is the amount to be raised for current budget deficit. While refinancing of redemptions is a matter of rolling over the same exposure as before, NBR refers to new exposure in the market.

- *The* funding *strategy* involves the choice of i) money market instruments for financing short-term GBR and ii) capital market instruments for funding long-term GBR. The strategy entails information on how borrowing needs are going to be financed using different instruments such as long-term, short-term, nominal, variable-rate, indexed bonds and FX-denominated debt.

- Gross *debt* corresponds to the outstanding debt issuance at the end of calendar years. This measure does not take the valuation effects from inflation and exchange rate movements, thus it is equal to the total nominal amount that needs to be paid back to the holders of the debt.

- Redemptions refers to the total amount of the principal repayments of the corresponding debt including the principal payments paid through buy-back operations in a calendar year.

Regional aggregates

- Total OECD area denotes the following 36 countries: Australia, Austria, Belgium, Canada, Chile, Czech Republic, Denmark, Estonia, Finland, France, Germany, Greece, Hungary, Iceland, Ireland, Israel, Italy, Japan, Korea, Latvia, Lithuania, Luxembourg, Mexico, Netherlands, New Zealand, Norway, Poland, Portugal, Slovak Republic, Slovenia, Spain, Sweden, Switzerland, Turkey, the United Kingdom and the United States. As most data in this chapter come from the 2019 survey all results which use the survey data exclude Colombia which only became the 37th member of the OECD on 28 April 2020.

- The G7 includes seven countries: Canada, France, Germany, Italy, Japan, United Kingdom and the United States.

- The OECD euro area includes 17 members: Austria, Belgium, Estonia, Finland, France, Germany, Greece, Ireland, Italy, Latvia, Lithuania, Luxembourg, Netherlands, Portugal, Slovak Republic, Slovenia and Spain.

- In this publication, the Emerging OECD group (i.e. OECD emerging-market economies) is defined as including five countries: Chile, Hungary, Mexico, Poland and Turkey.

- The euro (€) is the official currency of 19 out of 28 EU member countries. These countries are collectively known as the euro area. The euro area countries are Austria, Belgium, Cyprus, Estonia, Finland, France, Germany, Greece, Ireland, Italy, Latvia, Lithuania, Luxembourg, Malta, the Netherlands, Portugal, Slovakia, Slovenia, and Spain.

Calculations and data sources

- Estimates that are presented as a percentage of GDP are calculated using nominal GDP data from the *OECD Economic Outlook,* June 2020.

- Debt is measured as the face value of current outstanding central government debt. Face value, the undiscounted amount of principal to be repaid, does not change except when there is a new issue of an existing instrument. This coincides with the original promise (and therefore contractual obligation) of the issuer. DMOs often use face value when they report how much nominal debt will mature in future periods. One important reason for using face value is that it is the standard market practice for quoting and trading specific volumes of a particular instrument.

- To facilitate comparisons with previous versions of the Outlook, figures are converted into US dollars using exchange rates from 1 December 2009, unless indicated otherwise. Where currency are converted into US dollars using flexible exchange rates, notes in figures and tables refer explicitly to that approach. Source: Refinitiv. The effects of using alternative exchange rate assumptions (in particular, fixing the exchange rate versus using flexible exchange rates) are illustrated in Figures 1.3 and 1.4 of Chapter 1 of the *Sovereign Borrowing Outlook, 2016.*

- All figures refer to calendar years unless specified otherwise.

- Aggregate figures for gross borrowing requirements (GBR), net borrowing requirements (NBR), central government marketable debt, redemptions, and debt maturing are compiled from answers to the Borrowing Survey. The OECD Secretariat inserted its own estimates/projections in cases of missing information for 2019 and/or 2020, using publicly available official information on redemptions and central government budget balances.

- Negative-yielding debt calculations in Figure 1.6 (Panel B) are based on all issuances and re-openings of fixed-rate bonds (i.e. data excludes: short-term instruments, indexed linked, floating rate instruments and strips). Data is sourced from Refinitiv.

- For Figure 1.8: Several central banks have become dominant holders of domestic government bonds, it should be noted that for Panel A, the United States, marketable treasury securities, excluding treasury bills, held by the Federal Reserve as a share of outstanding marketable treasury securities, excluding treasury bills, at market value. For the United Kingdom, Asset Purchase Facility holdings as a share of outstanding (conventional) gilts, at market value. For Canada, government bonds, excluding treasury bills, held by the Bank of Canada as a share of outstanding Canadian government bonds. For Japan, government bonds held by the Bank of Japan as a share of outstanding treasury securities, excluding treasury discount bills and including FILP bonds, at nominal value. For the euro area countries, cumulative net purchases of government bonds in the Eurosystem Public Sector Purchase Programme and the Pandemic Emergency Purchase Programme at book value as of end-May 2020 as a share of outstanding general government bonds at face value as of end-April 2020. For Sweden, the purchases of government bonds (355.4 billion SEK as of15 May 2020) as a share of outstanding government bonds as of end-April 2020, at face value.

Notes

[1] This publication would normally standardise gross borrowing needs for short-term borrowing short-term operations, in order to make meaningful estimates that are comparable across the OECD area and also include comparable refinancing operations with corrections for artificially inflated (OECD, 2014[6]). In standardised gross borrowing needs, short-term gross borrowing requirements are calculated as the total of short-term debt stock at the end of the previous year and short-term net borrowing over the calendar year. This methodology aims to exclude funding needs (usually for cash management operations) for less than one year. However on this occasion gross borrowing figures are also presented as economies continue to issue debt in response to the ongoing COVID-19 pandemic.

[2] In Germany, the clause for exceptional circumstances in the public debt break was triggered on 25 March to allow debt financing of a supplementary budget of EUR 156 billion (4.5% of GDP) to cope with the coronavirus pandemic. An additional package for 2020 and 2021 of EUR 130 billion (3.8% of GDP) announced in early June is aimed at stimulating demand during the recovery (OECD, 2020[1]). Further off-balance liquidity support has been provided to firms, such as credit programmes through the national development bank (KfW), credit guarantees and equity injections. This contributed to increase in the 2020 financing and liquidity requirements of the Federal government's budget and its special funds.

[3] Sometimes, the institutions providing social transfers have issued bonds with state guarantees (e.g. UNEDIC in France). In other cases, extra expenses for social transfers were covered by changing the composition of expenditure, using emergency funds already attributed (e.g. Japan, South Korea).

[4] OECD Economic outlook assessed the impact of the fiscal responses on public debt levels under two different scenarios, namely single-hit and double-hit scenarios. Between 2019 and 2021, public debt relative to GDP in the OECD area is projected to increase by 18 percent under single hit scenario. The ratio increase by another 8 percentage points under double hit scenario (OECD, 2020[1]).

[5] EU initiatives in response to the crisis include the following: i) 'European Stability Mechanism (ESM) Pandemic Crisis Support' which is a low conditionality credit line that euro area countries can access to receive loans of up to 2% of their 2019 GDP and at a maturity of up to ten years; ii) 'The European Investment Bank's pan-European guarantee fund' amounts to EUR 25 billion to facilitate up to EUR 200 billion of loans primarily to SMEs; iii) 'A temporary Support to mitigate Unemployment Risk in an Emergency (SURE) programme', aiming to fight unemployment in the Union; iv) 'The European Commission recovery fund' plan to reinforce the EU budget with an exceptional and temporary EUR 750

billion fund, comprising around EUR 450 billion of grants, EUR 50 billion of guarantees and EUR 250 billion of loans, distribution of which are expected in early 2021.

[6] While majority of OECD sovereign issuers are anticipating changes in issuance size, a few countries including Lithuania, Poland, and Slovenia have reported no change in issuance strategies.

[7] The US Treasury, facing increasing funding needs already before the COVID-19 outbreak, consulted with a broad range of market participants regarding a set of instruments, including 20-year bonds, 50-year bonds and a SOFR index floating rate note in 2019. Their outreach suggested that there was stronger appetite for a potential 20-year bond, than for an ultra-long bond, as evidenced by their decision in to proceed with a new 20-year offering in 2020.

[8] A post-auction option is a facility whereby all successful direct bidders – mostly primary dealers – are offered the right to purchase up to an additional percentage of the securities they bought at the relevant auction, at the published average accepted price in multiple price format auctions.

[9] For example, 10-year bond yields dropped by 220 basis points on average in the OECD area between 2012 and 2019. Even though sovereign debt levels remained high in the OECD area, interest payments in relation to GDP have decreased due to issuance of debt at low interest rates during this period. On average interest expenses on general government debt as a percentage of GDP fell from 2.5% in 2012 to 1.8% in 2017 and further to 1.5% in 2019

[10] A 2017 survey of OECD Working Party on Debt Management (WPDM) members on alternative approaches to sovereign borrowing reveals that, when an alternative borrowing instrument is introduced, sovereign issuers consider a list of parameters: i) potential impact on existing instruments; ii) additional costs due to novelty and liquidity premia; iii) strength and sustainability of investor demand across interest rate cycles; iv) expanding investor base; v) complications around pricing of a new instrument; vi) portfolio diversification and risk reduction; vii) governmental decisions; viii) playing a leading role in developing a market segment (OECD, 2018[5])

2. Emerging market government securities: Long-term trends and developments since the pandemic

Over the last few decades, sovereigns of emerging market and developing economies have increasingly turned to capital markets to meet their financing needs. With the growth in marketable debt and supported by strengthened macroeconomic frameworks, local bond markets have deepened and public debt management capacity has improved in many of these economies. Drawing on the lessons learned from the several previous sovereign debt crises, many countries have also made important improvements in their public debt risk management systems. Despite these advances, the COVID-19 pandemic has demonstrated that sovereign debt markets for emerging economies are still highly vulnerable to global risks.

Using transaction level data from 107 countries, this chapter examines issuance trends of government securities in emerging market and developing economies since 2000. It first looks at currency, rating and maturity composition of debt issuance from 2000 to 2019. It then provides novel insights about the impact of the COVID-19 pandemic on debt issuance conditions for these countries.

2.1. Introduction

Over the last few decades, sovereigns in emerging market and developing economies have increasingly turned to financial markets to meet their financing needs, with consequent growth in marketable debt.[1] In particular, local currency bond markets, despite room for improvement, have deepened over the last decade, helped by a favourable global funding environment. As advisory efforts of multilateral institutions have increased and broadened significantly, public debt and risk management capacity has improved in many of these economies thanks to the lessons learned from the several previous sovereign debt crises, and improved macroeconomic frameworks. Nevertheless, emerging economies' sovereign debts are still highly vulnerable to global risks, as recent developments have shown. The COVID-19 pandemic has led to extraordinary volatility in the components of debt dynamics including economic growth, interest rates, and exchange rates in emerging market and developing economies, in addition to the surge in governments' borrowing needs.

Against this backdrop, this chapter presents an overview of issuance trends in emerging market and developing economies (hereafter 'emerging markets' or 'EMs') governments' securities, from 2000 to 2019 and provides novel insights about the impact of the COVID-19 pandemic on emerging markets debt issuance conditions. The chapter uses a dataset comprising a total of 83 695 sovereign government securities issued by 107 countries between January 2000 and May 2020 (see annex for details of the methodology used).

Key findings

- Annual gross issuance of central government securities by emerging market and developing economies has more than doubled from less than USD 1 trillion in 2000 to around USD 2.5 trillion in 2019. Total issuance of securities by emerging market sovereigns was USD 37.4 trillion between 2000 and 2019, almost three quarters of which has been issued since the 2008 financial crisis.

- Regional composition of EM debt has changed significantly over the past two decades. While the share of Latin American and the Caribbean region in total issuance has halved, China has become the largest issuer by nearly tripling its share. Both the MENA region and Emerging Asia have more than doubled their shares and Sub-Saharan Africa has quadrupled its share since 2000.

- On average, domestic currency issuance by EM sovereigns account for 90% of total issuance between 2000 and 2019, reflecting deeper local currency bond markets. At the regional level, currency composition has leaned gradually towards local currency in Emerging Asia over the period, while foreign currency issuance in Sub-Saharan Africa and MENA countries has increased notably in recent years.

- In terms of maturity profile, sovereign issuers with investment grade credit ratings succeeded in lengthening the average maturity of their issuance from 2000 to 2019, whereas market conditions have been more volatile for non-IG issuers, with maturities shortening somewhat over the same period. Overall, refinancing risk has increased as the share of total outstanding debt due in the next three years has increased more than 20 percentage points over the last two decades and was 33% in 2019.

- Since the 2008 financial crisis, EM sovereign credit ratings have drifted downwards. Specifically, EMs received a total of 401 downgrades, compared to 240 upgrades between 2008 and 2019.This trend has accelerated since the COVID-19 outbreak. There was 42 downgrades in the first five months of 2020, compared to the highest full-year total of 44 in 2016 and 2017.

Among the different rating categories, B-grade sovereign issuers have seen the majority of the downgrades since the outbreak of the COVID-19 pandemic.

- The pandemic initially caused sharp fluctuations in capital flows to EMs, leading to deterioration in borrowing conditions, though to different extents, among different country groups. In total, EM sovereigns raised more than USD 1 trillion in financial markets between January-May 2020, 19% higher than the historical average over the same period. Upper middle-income countries accounted for 56% of the total issuance, low middle-income countries for 29%, and low-income countries (LICs) only for 0.5%.

- Suffering from a flight to safety and consequent decreased investor interest, low-income issuers have been hit hardest by the pandemic. In the first five months of this year, the net amount of bond issuance by LICs, was around two-thirds of the previous five years' average. Moreover, they have significantly increased their dependence on short-term debt during this period.

2.2. Issuance of marketable debt by emerging market economies from 2000 to 2019

The importance of debt markets for emerging market sovereigns has increased significantly over the past two decades. From 2000 to 2019, annual issuance of central government securities more than doubled from less than USD 1 trillion to over USD 2.5 trillion (Figure 2.1). In particular, local currency bond markets have improved significantly over the last decade, helped by the favourable global funding environment. At the same time, multilateral institutions have stepped up their local currency bond market (LCBM) advisory efforts through various programs and initiatives (IMF WB, 2020[1]). Policymakers in several EMs have introduced macroprudential tools, improved public debt and risk management capacity and financial regulations that underpin the development of local currency bond markets in many of these economies in view of the lessons learned from the several sovereign debt crises (Kose, 2020[2]). At the same time, many EMs with chronic and high inflation history have gained inflation credibility by successfully implementing inflation targeting regimes. Both the prolonged economic expansion experienced in EMs over the last decade and the change in monetary regimes behind inflation stabilisation have contributed to the dissipation of 'original sin' (Ottonello and Diego, 2019[3]). Nevertheless, the sustainability of rapidly growing issuance amounts has been vulnerable to the risk of shifts in global risk sentiment.[2] In both gross and net terms, annual issuance of emerging market securities contracted considerably in 2003, 2008, and 2015.[3]

Despite a relative decline in gross issuance over the past three years, central government borrowing on public debt markets remains substantial. The low interest rate environment following monetary easing from major central banks and consequent low returns on advanced economy sovereign bonds have led to increasing availability of debt capital flowing to emerging and developing economies. Net issuance, which indicates new exposures in the market, has been positive in every year over the period, even during the GFC.

In total, governments of emerging and developing economies raised USD 37.4 trillion of debt from the markets between 2000 and 2019, almost three-quarters of which was issued since the 2008 financial crisis. In terms of security types, bonds were the primary form of issuance during the period analysed, while the use of short-term instruments has increased significantly, especially in recent years. Specifically, bonds accounted for 64% of annual issuance on average during the 2000-2019 period, albeit the share considerably decreased from 74% in 2000 to 62% in 2019 (Figure 2.1). In terms of interest rate composition, the proportions of fixed rate, zero coupon and floating rate issues were 49%, 43%, and 8%, respectively.

Figure 2.1. Gross and net annual sovereign debt issuance amounts in EMs (2019 USD, trillion)

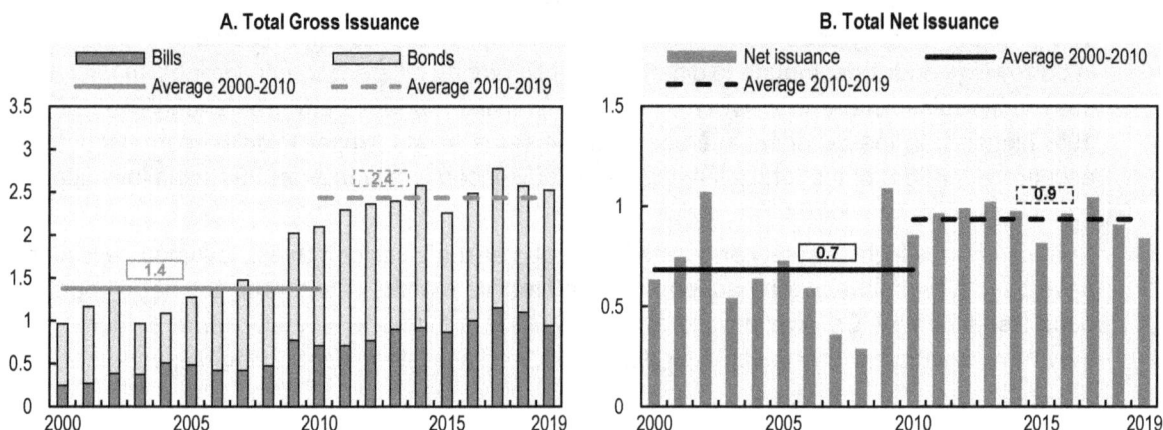

Source: OECD calculations based on data from Refinitiv.

Since 2000, the regional composition of EM debt has changed significantly (Figure 2.2). Emerging Asia accounted for the highest share of issuance in 2019. The region increased its issuance from 19% in 2000 to 44% in 2019. During the same period, China nearly tripled its share of total emerging economy issuance. Even excluding China, where the debt build-up has been particularly pronounced, debt issuance in Emerging Asia has risen to record highs. Also, the MENA region has more than doubled its share. The largest relative increase has taken place in Sub-Saharan Africa, which has quadrupled its share since 2000, reaching 8% in 2019. A corresponding decrease has taken place primarily in the Latin America and the Caribbean region, where the share decreased from 51% to 24%. It should be noted, however, that Brazil and Mexico have remained among the top five issuers.

Figure 2.2. Regional composition of emerging market sovereign debt issuance

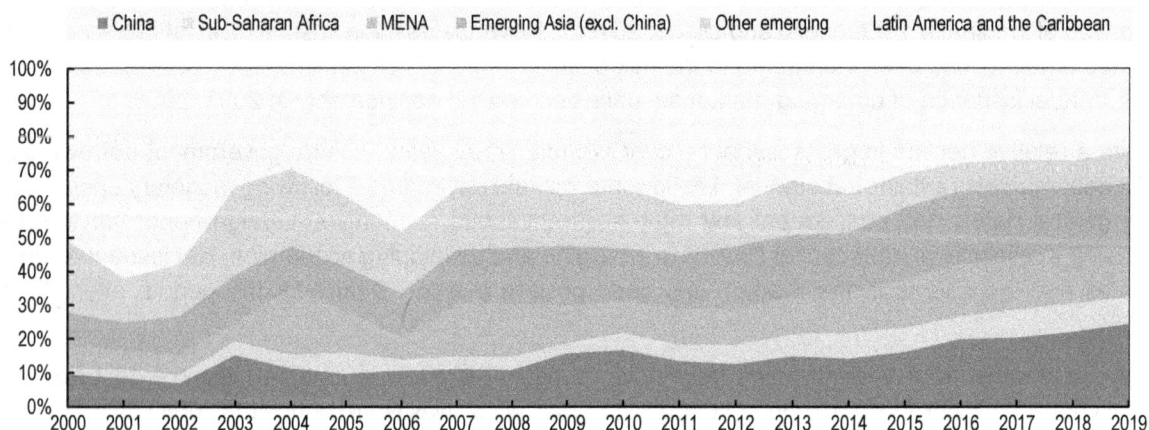

Source: OECD calculations based on data from Refinitiv.

2.3. Issuance trends in sovereign marketable debt

2.3.1. Currency composition of debt issuance

On average, domestic currency issuance by emerging economies accounted for 90% of total issuance between 2000-2019 (Figure 2.3). In particular, between 2007 and 2012, the ratio rose to 95% and started falling afterwards. When excluding bills the 2000-2019 average is 87%, reflecting the larger share of domestic currency issuance in short-term debt. A closer look at regional data reveals that Emerging Asia accounts for the largest share of the local currency bond market. Even excluding China, where foreign currency issuance has been negligible, share of local currency issuance in Emerging Asia has increased significantly over the past two decades. Contrarily, Latin America and the Caribbean, Sub-Saharan Africa and MENA increased the share of foreign currency issuance over the period, albeit with significant volatility between years.

Increasing share of local currency debt, especially in Emerging Asia, suggests deepening of local currency bond markets and an improvement in currency risk exposures in EMs where sudden reversals of capital flows have caused several debt crises in the past.[4] Deepening the financial market in a given country contributes to its ability to withstand volatile capital flows, helps reduce current account imbalances and reduces the reliance on foreign borrowing and the risks linked to currency mismatch (IMF WB, 2020[1]). Clearly, it is relevant for public debt management. A debt management strategy, building benchmark programs and liquid government securities, can contribute to development of local markets. At the same time, a deepening of local bond markets can improve the ability of the government to prepare a forward-looking debt management strategy and manage market risks. More generally, an increased local currency share in debt reduces the currency mismatch of the sovereign balance sheet, and the impact of currency fluctuations on debt service. However, it should be noted that build-up of private debt may pose a significant exposure risk to EMs if the private debt turns public through government interventions, especially if it is largely denominated in a foreign currency.

The distribution of bond ownership among different categories of investors may also be an important factor contributing to vulnerabilities in global capital flows.[5] Recent empirical studies indicate that the increase in local currency denominated securities has been accompanied by a growing share of debt held by non-resident investors (Arslanalp and Tsuda, 2014[4]). The share of non-resident investors' holdings in EM sovereign debt has grown significantly since the global financial crisis and reached 43 percent in 2018 (Kose, 2020[2]). In Emerging Asia, for example, the share of foreign holdings of local currency sovereign bonds reached 39% in Indonesia, and over 25% in the Philippines and Malaysia (ADB, 2020[5]). In addition to the deepening of local currency debt markets in EMs and the inclusion of bonds issued by some sovereigns in benchmark bond indices, the search for yield among investors that is driven by low interest rates in advanced economies has also contributed to this development.[6] However, it should be noted that high shares of debt held by non-resident investors might cause exchange rates of those EMs to depreciate more, as investors flee to safety in global sell-off episodes (Borris, 2018[6]; Hofmann, Shim and Shin, 2020[7]).

As illustrated in Figure 2.4, the US dollar has remained the dominant foreign currency between 2000 and 2019. With the euro, the two major currencies have made up an average of 97% of annual foreign currency issuance in emerging economies over the period. The third largest foreign currency is the Japanese yen, which has averaged 2.1%.

Figure 2.3. Share of foreign currency bonds in total sovereign debt issuance by region

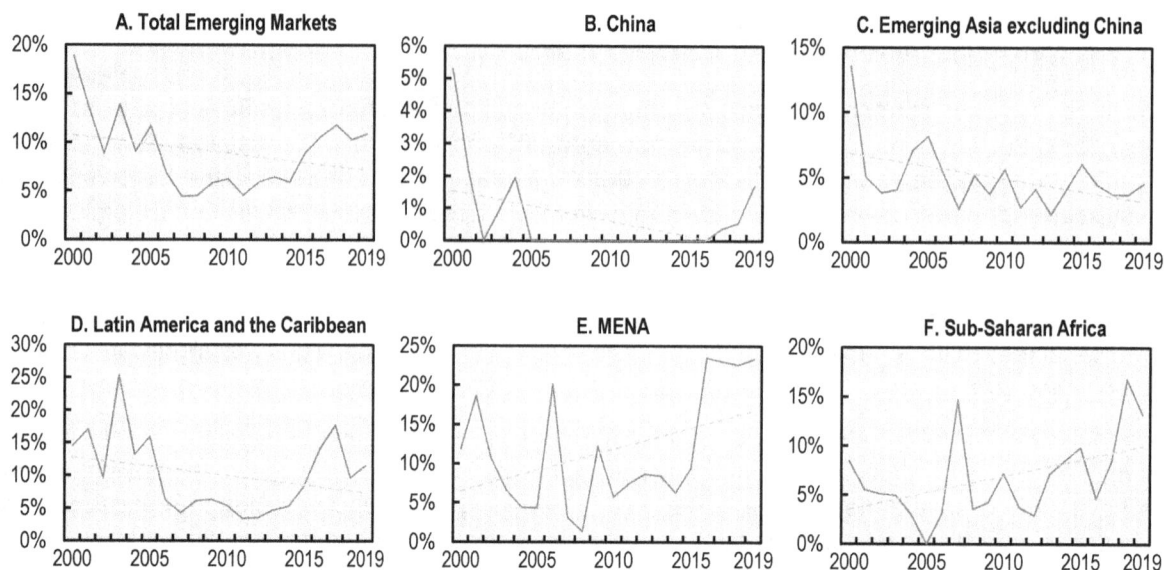

Source: OECD calculations based on data from Refinitiv.

Figure 2.4. Currency composition of emerging market foreign currency sovereign issuance by year

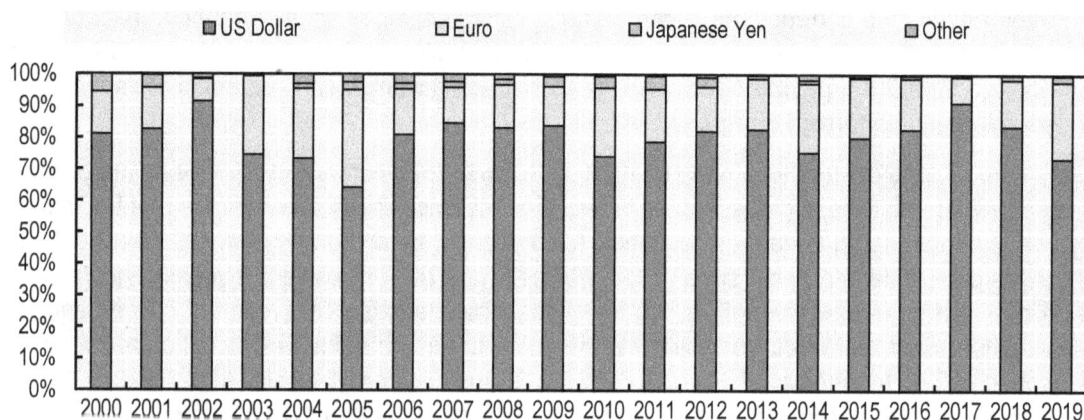

Source: OECD calculations based on data from Refinitiv.

2.3.2. Average maturity of sovereign debt issuance and refinancing risk

While sovereigns in EMs have increased their borrowings from the financial markets, term-to-maturities of sovereign debt issuance have been quite volatile, with the average of 5.5 years in the period under review (Figure 2.5). Issuance maturities are usually affected by liquidity conditions in global financial markets as well as macroeconomic conditions in the issuer country. A closer look at maturities by rating categories reveals different trends for investment and non-investment grade issuers. Sovereign issuers with investment grade managed to lengthen the average maturity of their issuance over the period from 2000 to 2019. On the other hand, maturity conditions have been more volatile for non-investment grade issuers, and somewhat deteriorated over the same period. The yearly average maturity of non-investment grade sovereign borrowing declined from 7.5 to 6 years between 2000 and 2019. At the height of the GFC in 2009 average maturity of issuance shortened to 3.1 years.

Figure 2.5. Maturity trends – average value weighted maturity, rolling 12 months

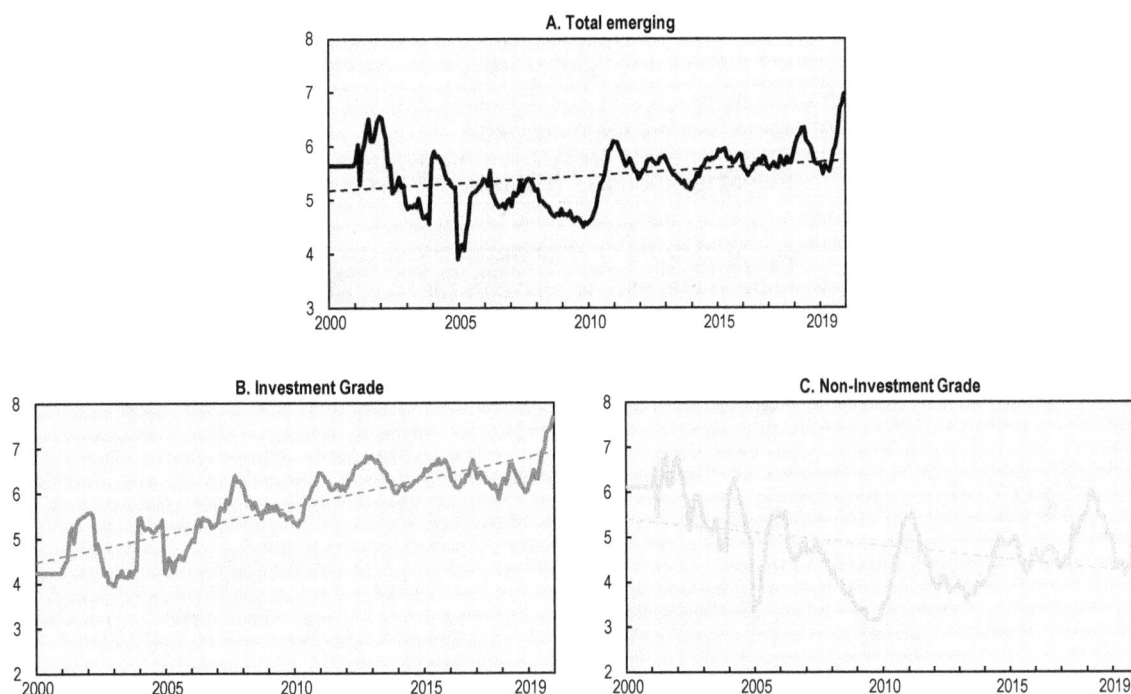

A. Total emerging

B. Investment Grade

C. Non-Investment Grade

Source: OECD calculations based on data from Refinitiv.

The significant increase in issuance of government securities with shorter maturities implies a cumulative increase in debt repayments and a challenging debt repayment profile. Figure 2.6 presents the share of outstanding amounts by region.

Figure 2.6. Outstanding amount of sovereign debt as of year-end 2019 by region

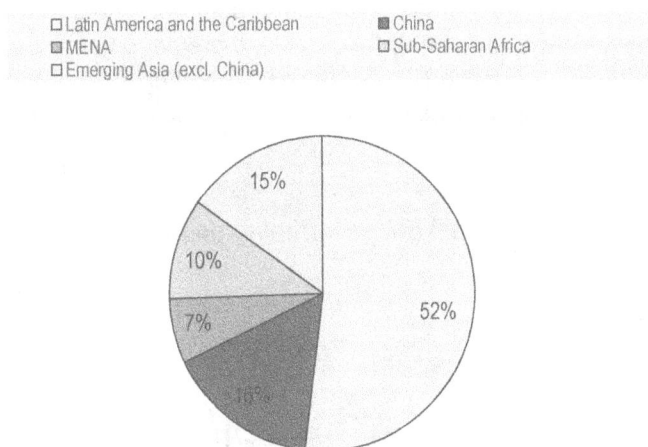

□ Latin America and the Caribbean   ■ China
■ MENA   □ Sub-Saharan Africa
□ Emerging Asia (excl. China)

52%

15%

10%

7%

Source: OECD calculations based on data from Refinitiv.

Figure 2.7 presents outstanding amount of government securities due within the subsequent three years as of the end of 2019. Debt due in the next three years as a share of total outstanding EM debt has increased by more than 20 percentage points over the last two decades, and was 33% in 2019. The ratio is much higher in LICs where debt due in the next 36 months was 41% in 2019. This increases the refinancing risk as many countries will seek to roll over their debts in the coming years. In the case of a continued low interest rate environment and ample global liquidity, governments may be able to secure cheap refinancing, but lower rated countries remain vulnerable to sudden stops in investor demand and flights to safety, as the COVID-19 pandemic has demonstrated.

Policy makers in EMs must also consider the amount of private sector debt coming due, taking careful note of potential crowding out issues as well as a source of implicit contingent liabilities. A recent study showed that non-financial companies in emerging markets need to repay or refinance USD 1.4 trillion within 3year years. The amount due within 3 years represents a record 50% of the total sum outstanding (Celik, Demirtas and Isaksson, 2020[8]).

Figure 2.7. Outstanding amount of sovereign debt due within 3 years as of end 2019

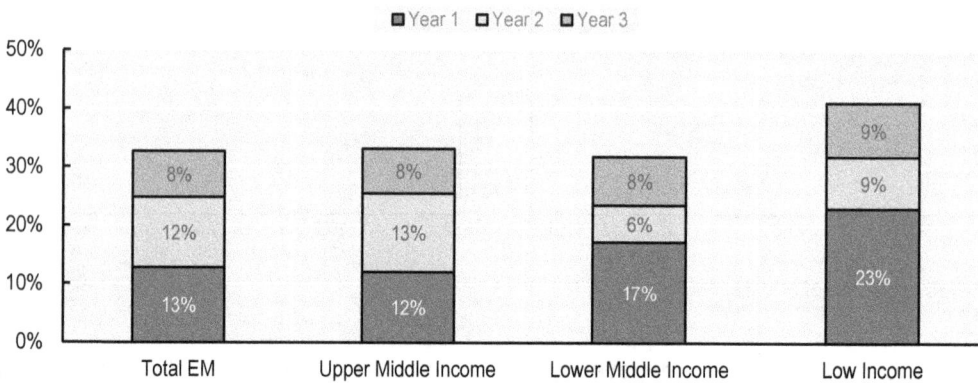

Source: OECD calculations based on data from Refinitiv.

2.3.3. Cost and credit quality of EM sovereign debt

An important contributing factor to the rise in EM sovereign debt has been the prolonged low interest rate environment, especially since 2008, which has encouraged both borrowers and lenders to take on more risk. While funding conditions have been broadly favourable, there have been several spikes in the market pricing of EM default risk during the period under review. A closer look at the yields on EM external government securities shows that bonds in the non-investment grade category, in particular CCC and lower graded sovereign bonds are more vulnerable to changes in global sentiment.

Figure 2.8. Yields and spreads on external EM government securities

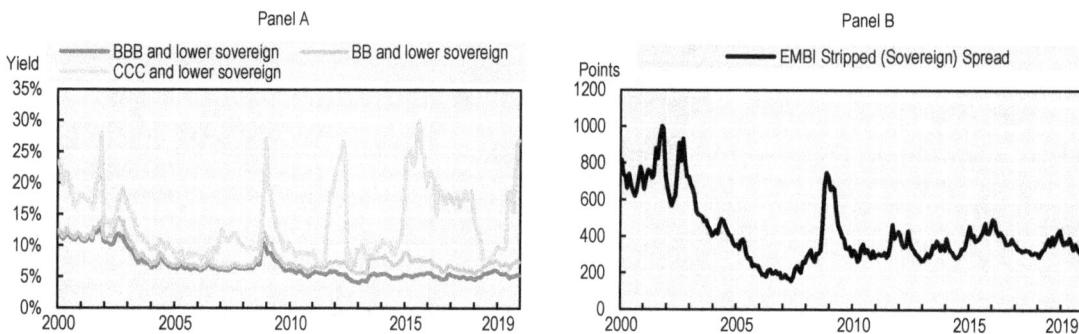

Source: Factset and Refinitiv.

In terms of credit quality, the share of investment grade bond issuance in total emerging economy issuances has more than doubled since 2000 (Figure 2.9). As of 2019, investment grade issuances made up 61% of total issuance in emerging economies. China plays a large part in this development. Its share of total rated issuance increased from 9% to 24% between 2000-2019. Since China has been rated investment grade throughout this period, this has a large impact on the below trend. However, even excluding China, the average share of investment grade issuance in emerging economies has increased from 40% in the 2000-09 period to 54% in the 2010-19 period. The improvement throughout the global financial crisis is both a reflection of the difficulty of non-investment grade countries to access debt markets and the fact that two new sovereigns were upgraded to investment grade in 2009 (i.e. Brazil and Peru).[7] However, it should be noted that, the search for yield continued to support higher-yielding, sub investment-grade emerging market bonds.

Figure 2.9. Share of investment grade rated bonds, and rating changes in total emerging market sovereign debt issuance

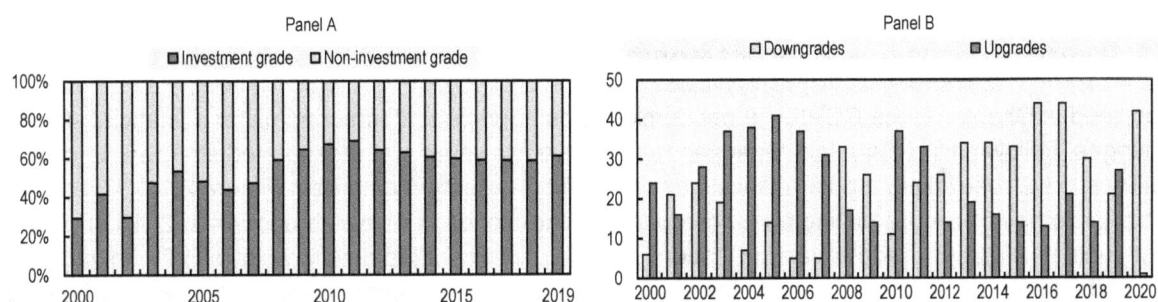

Source: OECD calculations based on data from Refinitiv.

Note: Above ratings are based on Moody's, S&P and Fitch and observed on a monthly basis, a change in rating by one agency is counted as 1 in the above chart, meaning that if all three agencies change their ratings in one month, it is counted as 3. When there is more than one change per agency in a month, the lower rating has been chosen, except in the case where the lowest rating is a default rating.

Emerging economies remain vulnerable to deterioration in global investor sentiment and global economic conditions. Sovereign credit ratings drifted upwards between 2000 and 2007. Between 2000 and 2007, a total of 252 upgrades (monthly observations) were given to emerging economies, two and a half times more than the 101 downgrades. The balance changed significantly after the GFC, after which downgrades significantly outpaced the upgrades. Specifically, emerging economies have received a total of 401 downgrades, compared to 240 upgrades since 2008.

The most important rating change is that on the threshold between investment grade and non-investment grade, since an investment grade rating can grant access to a significantly expanded pool of investors operating with risk restrictions. For example, a number of countries including Bulgaria, India, Kazakhstan and Russia obtained investment grade status in 2004 and thus gained access to a considerably wider pool of potential investors. Similarly, going from investment grade to non-investment grade (so-called "fallen angels") can lead to a significant contraction in available capital. Using the same methodology, Figure 2.10 Panel A shows the development in movements around that threshold. The number of downgrades to non-investment grade was particularly high in 2002, 2012, 2016 and 2017. As of December 2019, BBB rated bonds constituted 51% of EM sovereign investment-grade issuance, averaging 59% over the 2000-2019 period. So far in 2020, only one emerging economy, South Africa, has been downgraded from investment grade to non-investment grade. The share of BB-rated bonds (the highest non-investment grade rating) in non-investment grade bond issuance, which decreased from 65% in 2000 to 47% in 2009, amounted to 54% in 2019.

Figure 2.10. Composition of the investment and non-investment grade categories

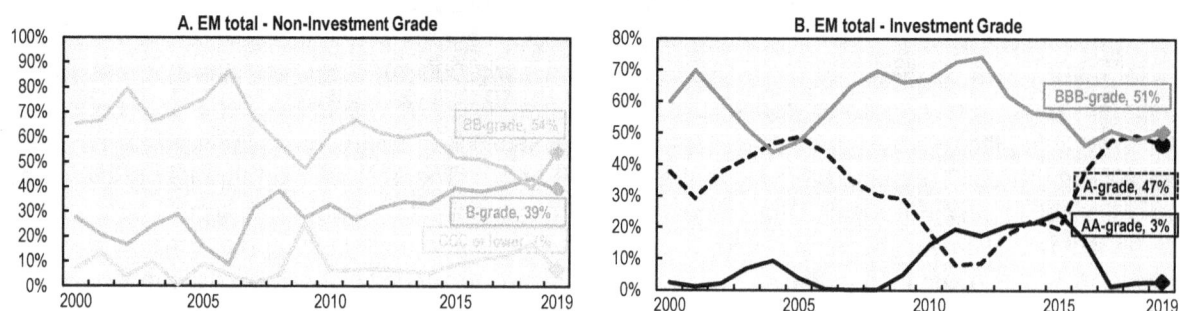

A. EM total - Non-Investment Grade

B. EM total - Investment Grade

Source: OECD calculations based on data from Refinitiv.

2.4. Initial impact of the pandemic on emerging sovereign debt markets

2.4.1. Issuance conditions in recent months

As outlined in Chapter 1, the COVID-19 pandemic poses unprecedented economic and financial stability challenges. Following the outbreak, emerging market investor sentiment deteriorated sharply and market volatility spiked, resulting in a poor financing environment for emerging markets (Figure 2.11). During this period, there have been 42 downgrades, compared to the highest full-year total of 44 in 2016 and 2017 (as of June 1st 2020). B-grade sovereign issuers saw the majority of the downgrades with 22 downgrades (52% of the total) within this category. In the analysed period, the number of downgrades per upgrade has never been higher than 3.4 (in 2016) and the average during 2000-2019 was 1.25. The first five months of 2020 were unique in that 42 downgrades were accompanied by only 1 upgrade (in January).

The demand for EM government bonds decreased sharply as investor risk aversion increased in March.[8] In particular, yields on CCC-rated sovereign bonds surged dramatically. As Panel A shows, the differential between average yields on CCC-rated sovereigns compared to BB-rated sovereigns began to narrow again following the sell-off in March and April, although the difference is still almost 20 percentage points.

Figure 2.11. Emerging market yield indices

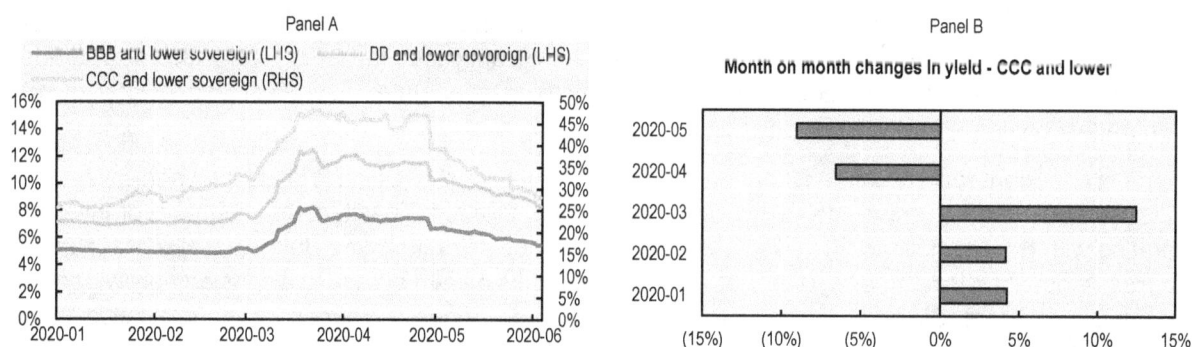

Panel A

Panel B

Month on month changes in yield - CCC and lower

Source: Bank of America ICE EM Indices, Refinitiv and Factset.

At the same time, in order to cope with the social and economic impact of the pandemic, several large EM economies have eased their monetary policy stance and announced fiscal measures which have increased borrowing needs. For example, several central banks have bought local currency government bonds to fight the effects of COVID-19, including Colombia, Indonesia, Mexico, Poland, South Africa, Turkey and the Philippines (OECD, 2020[9]). Further policy responses are expected, depending on the duration and magnitude of financial market stress, the impact of lower oil prices, negative international demand spillovers, domestic disruptions due to the pandemic, the extent to which vulnerabilities have built up before the crisis, and the policy space available to mitigate the negative shocks (OECD, 2020[10]). So long as global economic growth remains fragile and uncertainty over debt sustainability in some emerging economies remains a focal point of investor concern, risks for emerging markets sovereign bond issuance continues to be elevated.

Against this backdrop, between January and May, EM sovereigns raised USD 1.2 trillion via issuance of securities in financial markets, 19% higher than the average issuance levels of the previous five years (Figure 2.12). The countries in the upper middle income category, a majority of which are investment grade borrowers, have had market access at reasonable rates and actively decreased their rollover risk. They increased the issuance of government securities, notably in March. In particular, although China was the first country to experience the COVID-19 outbreak, it was able to tap domestic markets to finance fiscal measures announced by the government to support economic recovery (e.g. infrastructure projects).

During this period, prevalence of foreign currency denomination has also increased. The share of foreign currency issuance in investment grade EM sovereign issuance jumped to 27% in April 2020, close to triple the average share for April between 2015 and 2019. Contrarily, for non-investment grade issuers it plummeted to below 7%, compared to an average of 24% between 2015 and 2019, reflecting a loss of international market access. It should be noted that while currencies of oil-importing economies have generally fared better in the current crisis, currencies of commodity-producing economies (such as Brazil, Colombia, Mexico, Russia, and South Africa) depreciated significantly against the US dollar in the first quarter of 2020. To help ease currency pressures, several countries signed or enhanced existing bilateral swap arrangements with major central banks (e.g. Australia, Brazil, Japan, Malaysia, Mexico, Korea, Singapore and Thailand).

Issuance by the countries in the lower middle-income category, mostly in the non-investment grade category, was slightly higher in the first five months of the year (9%) than the historical averages, despite rising interest rates. From the perspective of the trade-off between funding cost and refinancing risk, lowering rollover risks takes priority over concerns about borrowing costs when there are large downside risks stemming from potential loss of market access.

Figure 2.12. Gross central government bond issuance by region and income group (USD, billions)

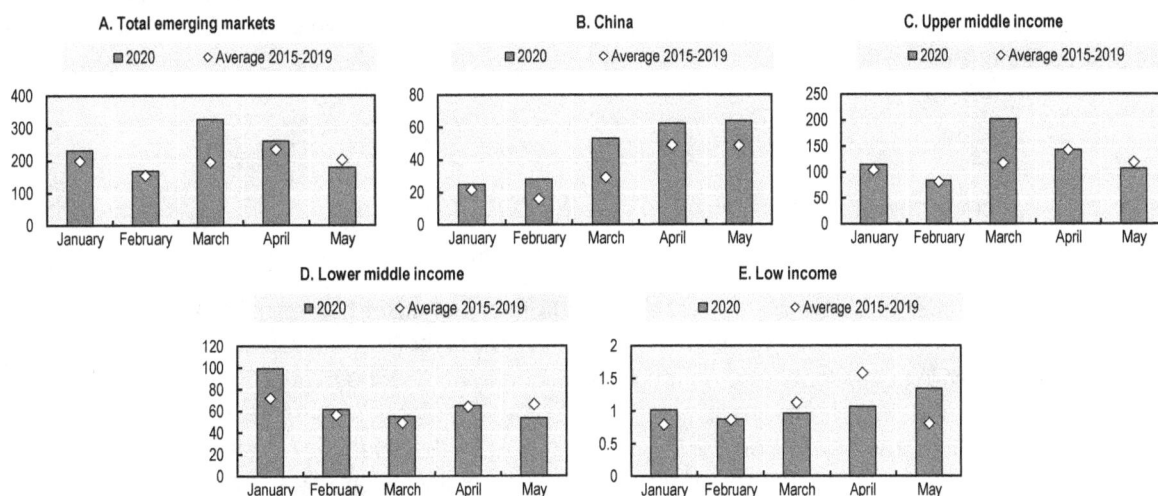

Source: OECD calculations based on data from Refinitiv.

In low-income countries, on the other hand, monthly issuance amounts were clearly below the historical averages during March and April, but improved in May. These countries, suffering from a flight to safety and consequent decreased investor interest, have been hit hardest by the pandemic.

In terms of net issuance, while the countries in the upper middle-income category have been able to issue significant amounts of new debt and thus increase net issuance, countries in lower middle-income and low-income groups have instead decreased theirs as a result of scheduled debt repayments in combination with lack of access to new borrowing.

Figure 2.13. Monthly net issuance by emerging markets sovereigns (USD, billions)

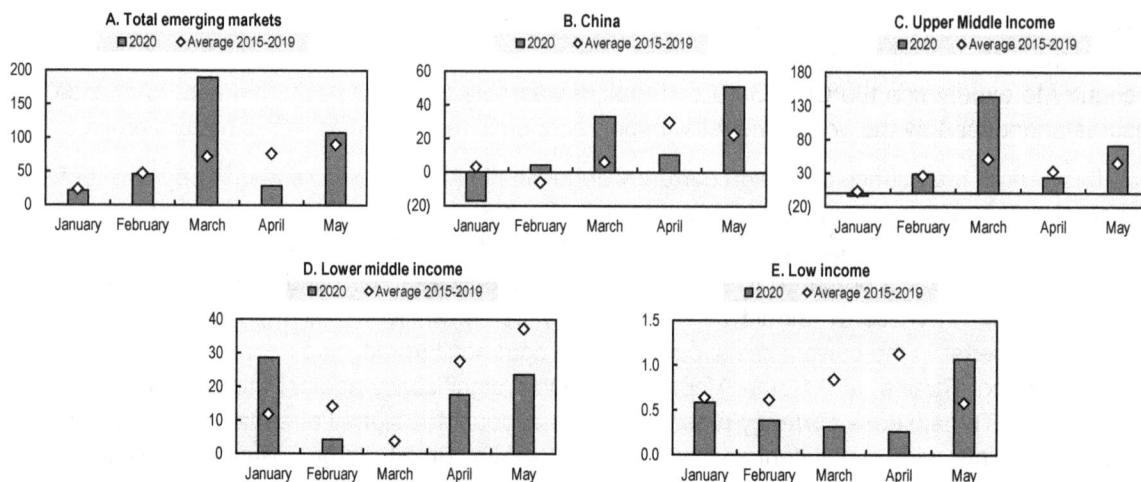

Source: OECD calculations based on data from Refinitiv.

The impact on the LICs, where the impact of COVID-19 has compounded with high debt levels, is of most significance. LICs issuance fell most sharply, despite a relative improvement in May. In the first four months of the year, the net amount of sovereign issuance by LICs was less than half of the previous five years' average. This suggests that some countries, with limited access to financial markets may be forced to limit macroeconomic policy support to weather the negative implications of the global recession. If the global economic downturn proves to be long-lasting, several of those countries could face downward revision of credit ratings and difficulty in repaying their existing debt to the markets, which would call for a need for debt restructuring (Box 2.1).

Box 2.1. Financing pressures in countries where the COVID-19 pandemic has elevated risk of debt stress

The debt build-up in emerging markets since the 2008 financial crisis has coincided with a period of slowing investment and productivity growth. Until recently, low global interest rates have mitigated near-term concerns over debt sustainability. Although institutions such as the World Bank and the IMF had raised alarms on the increasing fragility of low-income developing countries, market conditions remained benign (IMF and World Bank, 2020[11]). The COVID-19 pandemic has raised concerns over high levels of sovereign debt and debt service in some emerging economies. With the global shock causing high risk aversion and low commodity prices, a flight to safety dynamic is unfolding in emerging markets. The number of downward revisions of sovereign credit ratings and capital outflows from

---

emerging markets has been unprecedented (at over USD 90 billion, according to the IIF (IIF, 2020[12])). Countries with underdeveloped domestic financial markets that until weeks ago enjoyed access to international capital markets might be unable to roll over their existing debt, or repay their debt to investors. Figure 2.12 indicates the dramatic decline in sovereign bond issuance in financial markets by LICs during the first quarter of the year in comparison with the previous five years' average. At the same time, maturities of borrowings from the markets have shortened significantly. Many LICs, already about 40 percent were in debt distress before the pandemic, have started facing difficulties in repaying their debt. This emerging risk calls for the attention of the international community.

Multilateral cooperation plays a key role in providing financial support to the countries facing heavy debt repayments. The OECD has urged leaders to consider a "highly-indebted poor countries initiative on steroids" (Gurria, 2020[13]). The IMF and World Bank have already taken important steps to help financially constrained countries (IMF, April 2020[14]). On 15 April, G20 countries agreed to a "debt service standstill" from official bilateral donors, providing some direct liquidity support to the poorest countries (i.e.73 low-income countries), to which 41 had formally applied by end of June. Private creditors, including banks and bondholders, were also called upon to voluntarily defer debt service to countries which request it, but none so far have made such request. The fear of losing hard-earned market access, of potential ratings downgrades, as well as cross-default clauses have led countries to be cautious in approaching their creditors under the DSSI. In addition, the IMF approved SDR 17 billion (USD 24 billion) of emergency financing for 66 countries in the form of new concessionary lending, and cancelled six months of debt service payments on IMF loans in 25 countries. These initiatives brought a significant amount of relief, yet temporary.

If the global economic downturn proves to be long-lasting, consequences for several LICs, and to some extent also middle-income countries, could be sizeable and they could become insolvent (Bolton et al., 2020[15]). While the immediate need is to provide urgent resources, it might be necessary to consider deeper restructuring of the debt on a case-by-case basis, should such strategies be pursued by highly indebted countries. Countries dependent on oil exports, other commodities, or tourism, are experiencing a considerable economic shock, and could see a large share of their population slip back into poverty. In addition, the global recession could, depending on how long it lasts, push debt levels beyond what can be sustained. Several affected countries, such as Zambia (whose main export, copper, experienced a 20% price decline), Ecuador (suffering from one of the worst outbreaks among developing countries), or Argentina (whose debt was already unsustainable before the COVID-19 shock) have already entered into negotiations with lenders to restructure their debt. The international financial community has an important role in ensuring temporary debt relief for vulnerable countries and avoid turning higher debt ratios into solvency problems (OECD, May 2020[16]).

2.4.2. Maturity of issuance

During the initial phase of the COVID-19 crisis, at a time of acute market distress, both investment and non-investment grade issuers increased their issuance in short-term money markets, almost all in local currency. In particular, non-investment grade issuers increased their T-bill issuance by 48% in the first five months of 2020 compared to the previous five years' average, whereas total non-investment grade issuance only increased by 3%.

While investment grade issuers gradually moved towards long-term bond issuance with the subsequent stabilisation in financial markets, brought about by monetary policy measures since end-March, bond issuance by non-investment grade issuers remained significantly lower than historical averages in April and May. If the global economic downturn proves to be long-lasting, and borrowing conditions deteriorate further, the repayment risks in non-investment grade issuers, in particular for those rated CCC or lower, would be exacerbated.

46 |

Figure 2.14. Emerging market gross issuance by maturity style (USD, billions)

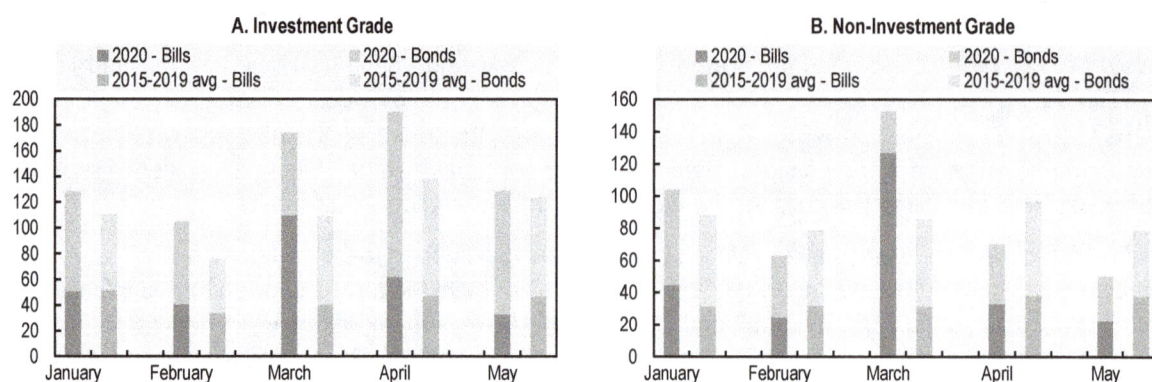

Source: OECD calculations based on data from Refinitiv.

References

ADB (2020), "Asia Bond Market Monitor", Asian Development Bank, https://asianbondsonline.adb.org/documents/abm_mar_2020.pdf?src=spotlight. [5]

Arslanalp, S. and T. Tsuda (2014), "Tracking Global Demand for Emerging Market Sovereign Debt", *IMF Working Paper*, Vol. No. 14/39, https://www.imf.org/en/Publications/WP/Issues/2016/12/31/Tracking-Global-Demand-for-Emerging-Market-Sovereign-Debt-41399. [4]

Bolton, P. et al. (2020), "Born out of necessity: A debt standstill for COVID-19", *CEPR, POlicy Insight*, Vol. NO. 103/April 2020, https://cepr.org/sites/default/files/policy_insights/PolicyInsight103.pdf. [15]

Borris, N. (2018), "Local currency systemic risk", *Emerging Markets Review*, Vol. 34/March 2018, https://doi.org/10.1016/j.ememar.2017.11.003. [6]

Celik, S., G. Demirtas and M. Isaksson (2020), "Corporate Bond Market Trends, Emerging Risks and Monetary Policy", *OECD Capital Markets Review*, http://www.oecd.org/corporate/ca/Corporate-Bond-Market-Trends-Emerging-Risks-Monetary-Policy.pdf. [8]

Ebeke, C. and A. Kyobe (2015), "Global Financial Spillovers to Emerging Market Sovereign Bond Markets", *IMF WP/15/141*, https://www.imf.org/en/Publications/WP/Issues/2016/12/31/Global-Financial-Spillovers-to-Emerging-Market-Sovereign-Bond-Markets-43035. [17]

Gurria, A. (2020), "What's At Stake: The Impact of COVID-19 on Developing Countries", *Written Statement to the Development Committee*, http://www.oecd.org/about/secretary-general/oecd-sg-written-statement-to-development-committee-imf-wb-2020.htm. [13]

Hofmann, B., I. Shim and H. Shin (2020), "Emerging market economy exchange rates and local currency", *BIS Bulletin*, Vol. 5, https://www.bis.org/publ/bisbull05.pdf. [7]

IIF (2020), "Capital Flows Tracker-The COVID-19 Cliff", Institute of International Finance, April, https://www.iif.com/Portals/0/Files/content/1_IIF_Capital%20Flows%20Tracker_April.pdf. [12]

IMF (April 2020), *Global Financial Stability Report*, https://www.imf.org/en/Publications/GFSR/Issues/2020/04/14/Global-Financial-Stability-Report-April-2020-49020. [14]

IMF and World Bank (2020), "The Evolution of Public Debt Vulnerabilities In Lower Income Economies", *IMF POLICY PAPER*, https://www.imf.org/en/Publications/Policy-Papers/Issues/2020/02/05/The-Evolution-of-Public-Debt-Vulnerabilities-In-Lower-Income-Economies-49018. [11]

IMF WB (2020), "Recent developments in local curecy bond markets in emergign economies", *Staff note for the G20 International Financial Architecture Working Group (IFAWG)*, http://documents.worldbank.org/curated/en/129961580334830825/pdf/Staff-Note-for-the-G20-International-Financial-Architecture-Working-Group-IFAWG-Recent-Developments-On-Local-Currency-Bond-Markets-In-Emerging-Economies.pdf. [1]

Kose, M. (2020), *Global Waves of Debt: Causes and Consequences*, The World Bank, https://www.worldbank.org/en/research/publication/waves-of-debt. [2]

OECD (2020), "OECD Covid-19 policy tracker", https://www.oecd.org/coronavirus/fr/. [9]

OECD (2020), *OECD Economic Outlook, Volume 2020 Issue 1*, OECD Publishing, Paris, https://dx.doi.org/10.1787/0d1d1e2e-en. [10]

OECD (May 2020), *A "debt standstill" for the poorest countries: How much is at stake?*, http://www.oecd.org/coronavirus/policy-responses/a-debt-standstill-for-the-poorest-countries-how-much-is-at-stake-462eabd8/. [16]

Ottonello, P. and J. Diego (2019), "The Currency Composition of Sovereign Debt", *American Economic Journal: Macroeconomics, 11 (3):174-208.*, http://dx.doi.org/10.1257/mac.20180019. [3]

Peiris, S. (2010), "Foreign Participation in Emerging Markets'Local Currency Bond Markets", *IMF WP/10/88*, https://www.imf.org/external/pubs/ft/wp/2010/wp1088.pdf. [18]

Reinhart, C. and K. Rogoff (2009), "The Aftermath of Financial Crises", *American Economic Review, American Economic Association*, Vol. Vol. 99(2), pp. pages 466-72. [20]

Ruch, F. (2020), "Prospects, Risks, and Vulnerabilities in Emerging and Developing Economies", *Policy Research Working Paper*, Vol. 9181, http://documents.worldbank.org/curated/en/787881584027048587/Prospects-Risks-and-Vulnerabilities-in-Emerging-and-Developing-Economies-Lessons-from-the-Past-Decade. [19]

Annex 2.A. Methodology for data collection and classification

Primary sovereign bond market data

Primary sovereign bond market data are based on original OECD calculations using data obtained from Refinitiv that provides international security-level data on new issues of sovereign bonds. The data set covers bonds issued by emerging market sovereigns in the period from 1 January 2000 to 31 May 2020 and includes both short-term and long-term debt. Short-term debt ("bills") are defined as any security with a maturity less than or equal to 367 days. The database provides a detailed set of information for each bond issue, including the proceeds, maturity date, interest rate and interest rate structure.

The definition of emerging markets used in the present report is the IMF's classification of Emerging and Developing Economies used in the World Economic Outlook. The regional definitions are also those used by the IMF, while the income categories used (low income, lower middle income, upper middle income) are defined by the World Bank according to GNI per capita levels.

A number of bonds have been subject to reopening. For these bonds the initial data only provide the total amount (original issuance plus reopening). To retrieve the issuance amount for such reopened bonds, specific data on the outstanding amount on each reopening date for the concerned bonds have been downloaded from Refinitiv. In order to obtain the issuance amount on each relevant date, the outstanding amount on a given date has been subtracted from the outstanding amount on the following date. The reopening data only provide amounts outstanding in local currency. The calculated issuance amounts are converted on the transaction date using USD foreign exchange data from Refinitiv. To ensure consistency and comparability, the same method is used for all bonds, including those which have not been subject to reopening.

Certain bonds in the dataset have been manually excluded when they did not have any identifier (ISIN, RIC or CUSIP) and when they have not been able to be manually confirmed by comparing with official government data.

Rating data

Refinitiv provides rating information from three leading rating agencies: S&P, Fitch and Moody's. For each country that has rating information in the dataset, a value of 1 to the lowest credit quality rating (C) and 21 to the highest credit quality rating (AAA for S&P and Fitch and Aaa for Moody's) is assigned. There are eleven non-investment grade categories: five from C (C to CCC+); and six from B (B- to BB+). The ratings data are observed on a monthly basis. In the case that a country has received several ratings in one month, the lowest one is used, except when that is a default rating (SD or D for S&P and RD or DDD for Fitch). The rating in question is then assigned to each relevant bond issued by that country. In the case that there are ratings available from several agencies, their average is used. When differentiating between investment and non-investment grade bonds, if the final rating is higher than or equal to 12 it is classified as investment grade. If the final rating is below 12 but higher than or equal to 11 and at least two agencies have given a rating higher than or equal to 12, it is also classified as investment grade. All other bonds are considered non-investment grade.

Income groups

The income classifications used in this chapter are the World Bank's Lending Groups and are based on GNI per capita levels. The countries in each group are listed below along with the GNI per capita thresholds.

Low-income economies (USD 1 305 or less)	Lower-middle-income economies (USD 1 306–4 045)	Upper-middle-income economies (USD 4 046–12 535)
Afghanistan	Algeria	Albania
Burundi	Angola	American Samoa
Burkina Faso	Bangladesh	Armenia
Central African Republic	Benin	Argentina
Chad	Bhutan	Azerbaijan
Democratic Republic of the Congo	Bolivia	Belarus
Democratic People's Republic of Korea	Cabo Verde	Belize
Eritrea	Cambodia	Bosnia and Herzegovina
Ethiopia	Cameroon	Botswana
Gambia	Comoros	Brazil
Guinea	Congo	Bulgaria
Guinea-Bissau	Côte d'Ivoire	China (People's Republic of)
Haiti	Djibouti	Colombia
Liberia	Egypt	Costa Rica
Madagascar	El Salvador	Cuba
Mali	Kingdom of Eswatini	Dominica
Mozambique	Ghana	Dominican Republic
Malawi	Honduras	Ecuador
Niger	India	Equatorial Guinea
Rwanda	Kenya	Fiji
Sudan	Kiribati	Gabon
Sierra Leone	Kyrgyzstan	Georgia
Somalia	Lao People's Democratic Republic	Grenada
South Sudan	Lesotho	Guatemala
Syrian Arab Republic	Mauritania	Guyana
Tajikistan	Federated States of Micronesia	Indonesia
Togo	Moldova	Iran

Low-income economies (USD 1 305 or less)	Lower-middle-income economies (USD 1 306–4 045)	Upper-middle-income economies (USD 4 046–12 535)
Uganda	Mongolia	Iraq
Yemen	Morocco	Jamaica
	Myanmar	Jordan
	Nepal	Kazakhstan
	Nicaragua	Kosovo
	Nigeria	Lebanon
	Pakistan	Libya
	Papua New Guinea	Malaysia
	Philippines	Maldives
	Sao Tome and Principe	Marshall Islands
	Senegal	Mexico
	Solomon Islands	Montenegro
	Sri Lanka	Namibia
	Tanzania	North Macedonia
	Timor-Leste	Paraguay
	Tunisia	Peru
	Ukraine	Russia
	Uzbekistan	Saint Vincent and the Grenadines
	Vanuatu	Saint Lucia
	Viet Nam	Samoa
	West Bank and Gaza Strip	Serbia
	Zambia	South Africa
	Zimbabwe	Suriname
		Thailand
		Tonga
		Turkey
		Turkmenistan
		Tuvalu
		Venezuela

Notes

[1] Marketable debt refers to financial securities and instruments that can be bought and sold in the secondary market such as bonds and bills.

[2] Among other factors, the inclusion of an emerging market economy into an index can trigger large portfolio reallocations. Emerging market bond indices, first introduced in 1990s, have rapidly expanded during 2000s with inclusion of a number of small and large issuers (e.g. from China and Mexico to Gabon, Ethiopia and Belarus).

[3] 2003, the impact of shifting interest rate expectations in major economies and a temporary heightening of risk aversion; 2008, the impact of the global financial crisis and 2015, a spill over from the Chinese stock market turbulence. Significant exchange rate volatility in some emerging market currencies affect the valuations, in particular in the early years of the analysed period.

[4] Several studies of EM crisis suggest that many crises began with sharp currency depreciations and capital outflows, where large depreciations increased service costs on foreign currency-denominated debt and complicated debt rollovers. Examples of debt crisis following a currency crisis include Mexico in 1994, East Asia in 1997, Russia, Argentina, and Turkey, in the late 1990s and early 2000s.

[5] The literature on foreign investor participation presents mixed results concerning the impact of foreign participation on financial markets. While foreign participation in local-currency sovereign bond markets provides an additional source of financing, reduces long-term government yields and helps the development of local bond markets (Peiris, 2010[18]), it raises concerns about increased sensitivity of yields to shifts in market sentiment and, even amplifying spillovers from global shocks (Ebeke and Kyobe, 2015[17]).

[6] Domestic government bonds issued in several EM economies are currently included in the widely used global bond indices. For example, Malaysia (2007), Mexico (2010), Poland (2003), Singapore (2005), and South Africa (2012) were included in Citigroup World Government Bond Index (WGBI).

[7] Brazil lost its final investment grade rating in 2016.

[8] It should be noted that this was a global phenomenon for distressed and close to default debt, which also includes BB and lower rated corporate debt in advanced economies. For example, the total issuance by non-investment grade corporations was less than USD 5 billion in March 2020, which is only 12% of the average amount issued in the same month during the past five years.

3. Governance of public debt in the times of a global crisis

The COVID-19 pandemic presents a historic challenge for sovereign debt management offices. In addition to operational challenges, liquidity and funding risks have escalated to unprecedented levels during the crisis. Debt management preparedness to respond to these challenges is critical for supporting both the efficacy of each government's emergency response and the smooth functioning of financial markets.

This chapter discusses how debt management offices of the OECD countries can adapt their governance practices to prioritise and deal with various aggravated operational and market risks in these times of a major crisis in order to achieve their objectives.

3.1. Introduction

The COVID-19 pandemic poses significant challenges for public debt management offices (DMOs) including i) sudden and significant increases in borrowing needs; ii) increased market volatility; iii) health and safety risks in workplaces; and iv) temporary mismatches in fiscal cash flows. Debt management preparedness to help respond to these operational, liquidity and funding challenges is critical for supporting both the efficacy of each government's emergency response and the smooth functioning of financial markets.

This chapter discusses how debt management offices of the OECD countries can adapt their governance practices to prioritise and deal with various operational and market risks during a global crisis, such as the COVID-19 outbreak.

Key findings

- In the midst of a severe crisis as the COVID-19 pandemic, ensuring the continuity of business is a priority to deal with other types of risks that a debt management office faces. The operational capabilities of DMOs should be ensured through taking measures concerning working arrangements (e.g. split operations, remote working, office distancing) to enable the handling of critical functions such as funding operations and debt repayments.

- As funding needs of governments have increased significantly and suddenly during the period of the crisis, coordination amongst the authorities in charge of budget planning, funding, liquidity management and financial stability have become more important. DMOs must coordinate closely with other government bodies, especially central banks and ministries of finance, to be able to react to changes in budget plans (e.g. unanticipated cash flows, authorisation to increase debt/borrowing limits) and market liquidity in a timely and effective manner.

- Markets become more sensitive and reactive in periods of stress, thus funding conditions can profoundly change in a short period of time. The key challenge is to increase issuance to finance the policy response, while avoiding a potential decline in market functioning.

- DMOs, as regular players, may want to consider prefunding future requirements (if possible) in case conditions deteriorate, closely monitor market developments and market participants to be able to adjust issuance strategies and procedures in a timely manner.

- Clear and timely communication of any adjustment to issuance programmes plays an important role in limiting uncertainty and reputational effects, and promoting market resilience. At the same time, strengthening communication with markets, especially with primary dealers, enables DMOs to gain a deeper insight into investor demand.

- In their role as regular and large issuers in securities markets, DMOs should carefully manage changes in borrowing programmes by balancing the need for transparency and predictability while allowing for sufficient room for manoeuvre.

- Contingency funding tools such as liquidity buffers, T-Bill issuance and credit lines with commercial banks can be used to mitigate unexpected variations in borrowing needs and avoid potential disruption to financing programmes, which in turn supports predictability in public debt management. Moreover, building additional flexibility, such as boosting cash buffers, providing flexibility at auctions, and allowing unscheduled adjustments to the issuance calendar will help governments to withstand surges in additional funding needs until long-term financing can be secured.

3.2. Operational challenges and ensuring business continuity during the pandemic

The COVID-19 pandemic has ignited significant health, social, economic and financial crises globally. In terms of business operations, it has had a profound impact on the ways people work due to social distancing (i.e. widespread remote work). Under this environment, ensuring business continuity of debt management offices (DMOs) has become vital for governments to respond to the pandemic effectively as they are responsible for raising funds to meet the governments' financing needs. The majority of DMOs in the OECD area regularly conduct business impact analysis of potential disruptions in business processes (in terms of economical and reputational consequences as well as governance), and have enhanced back-up systems in place to handle critical functions such as funding operations and debt repayments (Box 3.1). Having a business continuity and recovery plan available to put into practice helps DMOs to quickly respond to operational challenges posed by the pandemic. At the same time, DMOs would benefit from reviewing of their pandemic preparedness in case of a prolonged period of confinement or a potential second-wave of infections.

Box 3.1. Business Continuity Planning in Debt Management Offices

Sovereign debt management offices (DMOs) are in charge of critical government activities such as raising funds to meet governments' financing needs and repayments of debt to investors. Therefore, almost all sovereign debt management offices in the OECD area have well-developed business continuity and disaster recovery plans to ensure their core business operations are maintained in in case of an emergency or an event risk.

A plan for business continuity typically outlines how an organisation will continue to function during and after an emergency or event. It involves identification of critical functions, key internal and external dependencies and contingency planning of how key services or products can continue under different scenarios. The main risks that are seen as having the potential to disrupt debt management operations at the primary site can be listed as follows: i) disruptions to - or failure of - information technology (IT); failure of global network systems used for communications; unavailability of databases and records; external suppliers (e.g. power, water, transportation); external threats (e.g. terrorism, natural disasters); disruptions to the financial system, and unavailability of staff (e.g. pandemic). As most of the threats involve facilities, external suppliers, and equipment, the contingency measures in place to mitigate risks to continuity of debt management operations at primary sites mainly cover backup power supply, communication, IT, data storage and recovery, protection of legal contracts. In the majority of cases, there has been a maximum downtime objective established at the primary site, which is typically very short for vital operations and longer for non-vital operations. Also, most DMOs in the OECD area have secondary sites as part of business continuity plans (BCPs) and would be able to resume business within approximately a half day following the invoking of the BCP.

Source: WPDM Survey of Business Continuity Plans of Debt Management Offices, 2006 and discussions held at the 2019 annual meeting of the WPDM.

Similar to other businesses, the pandemic affects business operations of sovereign debt management offices in terms of health and safety of workers. At the same time, the fiscal response to the pandemic has led to a surge in borrowing needs of governments, which in turn has increased the need for funding and cash management activities of DMOs. In this context, many DMOs have activated their BCPs at early stages of the outbreak to ensure their critical functions (government financing and debt repayments) are resilient during the crisis. If a BCP is not available, simple measures can be taken to ensure business continuity by identifying critical processes and developing a remote working plan as described below.

Sovereign debt management encompasses highly technical tasks such as funding, liquidity management, risk management, and settlement and payments that require a high degree of financial expertise and experience. Unlike other potential threats to operations, a pandemic may prevent workers from returning to work in full capacity for what can be a prolonged period of time. Also, workers or family members can be affected and unable to take part in work activities. Therefore, ensuring business continuity during a pandemic requires not only remote access to the workplace but also health and safety of human resources for longer outages. It is important to note that building nationwide resilience at a broader level and employing a strong internal risk control environment at a granular level to deal with these risks are important features of efficacy of risk management measures. These measures are as follows:

- Create a pandemic management team that assigns roles and implements business continuity plans to ensure that the critical business activities remain operational for several weeks or months with limited staff
- Heightened hygiene at workplace (e.g. provide hand sanitizers, disinfection of the workspace and meal planning)
- Establish split operations (clean team), assess division of labour in terms of critical activities; and ensure effective communication both within and across teams
- Develop methods to conduct your business remotely (e.g. remove manual approval processes for funding operations and repayments; allow workers to use flexible work options; develop communication methods to reach all staff, and; enhance technology and communications equipment and relevant protocols)
- Assess and plan for downsizing services (e.g. non-critical operations such as research activities, derivative operations), and also anticipate a surge in some operations (e.g. funding operations, cash management and investor relations)
- Redesign office layout to ensure social distancing at the work place (e.g. limiting number of staff per office, establishing physical barriers, no-visitor policy)
- Cross train more staff with critical skills through virtual classes and webinars to avoid key person risk (e.g. staff involved in cash market operations, derivative markets and debt repayments)
- Consider replacing face-to-face meetings (including internally) with online meetings
- Make sure key counterparts, in particular primary dealers, have put in place a well-developed business continuity and disaster recovery plan that includes pandemic preparedness
- Develop partnerships with stock exchanges, financial and other clients, the treasury, the central bank, the clearing house and the depository, in order to coordinate activities to meet the recovery time objectives
- Be vigilant against heightened risk of cyberattacks during the pandemic

It should be noted that remote work also imposes challenges to businesses. Information security, privacy and timely technical support can cause delays. It might affect the promptness of the operations in the financial sector similar to many other sectors of an economy. Therefore, in addition to the above listed measures, DMOs would benefit from being mindful about the impact of remote working conditions in other businesses across the world. In view of this, DMOs might consider providing flexibility to primary dealers with respect to their reporting and market obligations (e.g. quoting obligations, flexibilities around deadlines and scope of reports) during the pandemic. Also, ensuring a close communication with primary dealers to keep the market's pulse and to understand investors' behaviour and motivations, and avoiding requesting additional research/reports are of the utmost importance.

Once the crisis is over, sovereign debt management offices should review their business continuity and recovery plans in light of the lessons learned during the COVID-19 crisis. Identification of gaps in BCPs or necessary equipment to be acquired would help to improve their preparedness for a pandemic risk. Furthermore, the use and priority of secondary sites might be worth reviewing as the recent experience of wide-scale remote working experience has proved to be effective in managing certain type of stress scenarios.

3.3. Stronger coordination with other authorities

Crisis conditions require strong coordination and communication amongst the relevant authorities to enable them to respond quickly and prudently. In this regard, the COVID-19 pandemic is not an exception. From a public debt management perspective, it requires a close coordination with fiscal and monetary policy authorities given the massive impact of the pandemic on fiscal projections, governments' immediate need for cash as well as on financial markets. In addition, a broader level of coordination is necessary to mitigate safety and health conditions of staff and to manage relevant operational risks, as discussed in the previous section.

The pandemic's economic impact in terms of shrinking domestic production, collapsing tax revenues, and ballooning fiscal deficits is visible worldwide. At the same time, governments need to spend unprecedented sums of money not just on healthcare and social interventions to fight COVID-19, but also on job guarantees and welfare payments. All of these weigh heavily on governments' budget projections and cash flow estimates: i) A combination of a drop in fiscal revenues and massive jump in fiscal spending poses a significant challenge for authorities to estimate short-term cash needs, in particular where a number of fiscal stimuli packages are announced in a short period of time; ii) Making realistic medium- and long-term cash flow estimates becomes extremely difficult given the uncertainty attached to fiscal projections, as well as global health and growth expectations. On the whole, this situation calls for strong coordination amongst the authorities in charge of public financial management such as tax and revenue administrations to estimate new fiscal cash flows and prioritise spending items.[1] The quality and timely delivery of cash flow forecasts have a crucial role in making informed decisions regarding the timing and size of funding, as well as use of safety nets. Anecdotal evidence suggests that sovereign debt managers quickly re-activated their emergency communication skills from the GFC, which has led to efficient sharing of information amongst relevant departments of ministries of finance.

The interaction between DMOs and central banks (CBs) regarding their policy moves is extremely important for the smooth functioning of government securities markets at all times. While the current crisis is increasing sovereign debt levels as well as government securities holdings of central banks, this new and complex environment requires stronger coordination between monetary policy and debt management authorities. Main issues require exchange of information between authorities of debt management and monetary policy where they are related to liquidity management, primary dealership system, investors' behaviour and yield curve movements. For example, DMOs usually issue T-Bills or make use of other safety nets such as cash buffers and credit lines to absorb sudden and sharp variations in cash flows to keep their bond issuance plans unchanged. Clearly, the choice of different financing strategies has different implications for liquidity conditions in the market, which is pertinent to monetary policy transmission. Another aspect of the interactions concerns primary dealers, who often act as intermediaries in flowing the liquidity and government securities into the economy.

In order to support markets and economic growth, major central banks in the OECD area have been deploying emergency interventions and providing a lot of liquidity to the economies. These include interest rates at or near the effective lower bound, embarking on massive securities-buying programs, reopening emergency financing windows and creating new ones. Clearly, these measures have implications for sovereign debt markets. First of all, swift action by central banks in the main advanced economies, in particular in the United States, has led to a massive increase in market liquidity, helping to ease stress in financial markets and minimise risks triggered by containment measures (OECD, 2020[1]). The resulting low interest rates and increased central bank holdings of government bonds have reduced government debt servicing costs significantly. In the euro area, for example, the ECB has allowed flexibility in other self-imposed restrictions (i.e. fluctuations in the distribution of purchase flows over time, across asset classes and among jurisdictions) and included debt securities with maturities (i.e. as short as 70 days T-Bills) into its new Pandemic Emergency Purchase Programme (PEPP) in March 2020. This in turn helped to ease funding conditions of the euro area sovereigns overall. In particular, it was helpful for sovereign DMOs that have issued T-Bills to build their cash buffers in the early phase of the crisis. The Bank of England, on the other hand, has provided the government with cash advances, through a temporary extension of the Ways and Means (W&M) facility to directly finance additional government spending.[2] From a monetary policy perspective, this temporary tool aims to avoid a tightening of monetary conditions due to governments' high borrowing requirements. From a debt management perspective, it helps the DMO to finance government's crisis measures without the need to turn to the markets which could be volatile.

If existing communication and coordination structures are deemed inadequate, formal protocols (e.g. memorandum of understanding) or changes in existing protocols (e.g. clear and strict instructions) for information sharing can be put in place with the relevant authorities.

3.4. Remaining vigilant against market developments in unprecedented times

Until the pandemic arrived, financial market conditions were buoyed by a general sense of optimism on the back of supportive monetary policies and reduced trade tensions. With the rapid spread of the virus, the outbreak turned into a global pandemic in a few weeks and uncertainty about global economic downturn crushed investors' expectations.[3] While investors became more risk averse, this flight to quality behaviour manifested itself as a sharp fall in the prices of risky asset and commodities; and a surge in the prices of safe-haven assets (Please see Chapter 1 for details). Thus, funding risk has been high on sovereign debt managers' agenda since the outbreak.

Monitoring market developments and having two-way communication with investors are essential for sovereign issuers to realise their objectives with respect to minimising debt service cost for a given level of refinancing risk and supporting well-functioning government securities market at all times. These are critical to enable debt managers to draw up more informed issuance strategies (i.e. aligning issuance plans with market demand) and to adjust investor relations and communication practice. Remaining vigilant against market developments and continuous communication with investors becomes even more important during times of crisis, where market conditions could change abruptly. In adverse market conditions, investors' appetites may switch to a risk-off mood and market liquidity can evaporate suddenly. This in turn can affect demand for government securities in primary markets. The risk-off mood can be exacerbated in the face of sudden rating downgrades and/or changes in outlook, especially if such actions occur off-calendar, thus elevating uncertainty levels going forward. If a severe market strain is foreseen, sovereign issuers can modify the timing and method of issuance. Otherwise, they might have to face less successful funding operations (e.g. uncovered auctions).

Until now, the increased borrowing has been relatively well absorbed by markets in major economies. This partly reflects the fact that many advanced countries benefited from a "flight to quality" effect as investors switched out of equity and other "risky assets". Also, large bond purchasing programmes deployed by major central banks have supported demand for government securities. However, similar to the GFC, issuance conditions have worsened in some markets with somewhat weaker demand at auctions in some jurisdictions, particularly during the initial phase of the crisis. It should be noted that these incidences can be read as "single market events" and not as unambiguous evidence of systemic market absorption problems. Debt managers have reported that they have been in interaction with primary dealers and other investors more frequently than before through emails, phone calls and virtual meetings.

Countries with limited fiscal space, high financing needs, or external financing vulnerabilities, including Hungary, Mexico and Turkey, have been more exposed to sudden changes in investor sentiment. Those countries should make use of safety nets, if available. If not readily available, they might benefit from building emergency cash buffers or establishing credit lines with commercial banks, or a short-term cash advance facility from central banks. In addition, when designing an issuance operations calendar, they should try to avoid potentially market moving data releases and other scheduled external events as far as known and practicable (e.g. major CBs' interest rate announcements, elections, major economic data releases. At the same time, it's important to maintain flexibility to be able to make minor adjustments to account for dates of major events announced after the issuance calendar. This provides an opportunity to communicate shifts in the auction calendar well in advance.

In the midst of a severe crisis such as this one, usual issuance mechanisms and procedures may not be fully effective. Consultation with primary dealers about issuance methods, auction calendars, and instruments choices could be valuable for successful management of stressed periods. For example, some investors might be less keen to participate in competitive auctions amid highly volatile market conditions. DMOs might benefit from putting in place a post-auction option facility (i.e. non-competitive subscription) or modifying design features of the facility to attract investors to auctions.[4] Specifically, availability of the facility can be expanded in terms of its size and investor groups (e.g. institutional investors and small investors). Similarly, investors might face difficulty in trading less liquid bonds (e.g. off-the-run-bonds). In order to support the functioning of the government securities markets, DMOs might consider introducing buy-back or switch facilities with eased conditions.

In addition, issuers should adapt their market monitoring practices as well as communication strategies to the pandemic. They can communicate directly and at less cost with investors through conference calls, web-based communications and social media. They should monitor markets more closely and more frequently.

Clear and timely communication of any adjustment to issuance programmes plays an important role in limiting uncertainty and reputational damage, and promoting market resilience. At the same time, strengthening communication with markets, especially with primary dealers, enables DMOs to gain a deeper insight into investor demand. Given the uncertainty in the economic outlook and increasing re-financing needs, the future might hold even more challenging funding conditions which might complicate the execution of borrowing programs. Existing issuance procedures, primary dealer arrangements, and portfolio management strategies may not work as efficiently as they did before the crisis. In this context, sovereign issuers may need to adapt their operations to the new conditions. For example, during periods of stressed market conditions, banks might face difficulties in participating in auctions or delivering market making activities as defined in the PD agreements.[5] If deemed necessary, DMOs should adjust implementation of primary dealership systems and ease primary and secondary market obligations of the intermediaries temporarily in view of the extraordinary circumstances.

3.5. Striking a balance between transparency and flexibility

Adherence to transparency and predictability is one of the key principles of debt management that enables sovereign debt management offices to achieve their objective of minimizing borrowing cost over the long-term.[6] This provides certainty for investors and intermediaries concerning the size and composition of the issuance of government securities, and results in better market functioning and liquidity (OECD, 2016[2]). Sovereign issuers provide predictability through disclosing their financing programmes by using annual, quarterly and monthly financing plans and other communication tools. Nevertheless, greater transparency reduces the flexibility of implementing financing plans. In their role as regular and large issuers in securities markets, DMOs need flexibility to follow their financing programmes, especially under extraordinary conditions when there is considerable uncertainty about borrowing requirements.

When flexibility is built into debt management policies, DMOs can take a proactive approach on several fronts including i) addressing unexpected funding needs with low cost, ii) preventing possible threats to the government's reputation and financing capacity due to failed auctions, and iii) easing market liquidity strains over certain bonds through buy-back or exchange operations (OECD, 2019[3])). Flexibility, aiming to support predictability, can be embedded into financing plans through contingency funding tools. These include the use of T-Bills, liquidity buffers, funding in foreign currencies, and credit lines with commercial banks. Considering the costs attached to them, these tools are designed to mitigate short-term liquidity risk and avoid potential disruption to financing programmes. Also, issuance techniques and pricing systems can also be adapted to market conditions. For example, DMOs might consider switching to a single-price auction temporarily to make pricing easier for investors.

In the case of a massive shock to borrowing needs, there may be situations where none of these measures is sufficient to avoid deviations from issuance plans. In the fight against the pandemic and its massive impact on economies and markets, governments across the world have introduced a number of fiscal packages. The fiscal response has been fast and significant, which required fundamental adjustments to governments' funding plans. In addition to enacted policy measures, the impact on the fiscal balance through automatic stabilizers can be significant, although its exact magnitude can prove difficult to project considering the specificity and unprecedented nature of the pandemic shock. Consequently, both size and composition of borrowing plans of many DMOs have had to change in just a few weeks. Going forward, given the uncertainties attached to the evolution of the pandemic as well as recovery in the global economy, when reviewing issuance plans, DMOs should assess different scenarios to estimate government borrowing needs, rather than strictly following a base-line estimation. Sovereign issuance schedules for the second half of the year, particularly in the countries most affected by the pandemic, are subject to considerable uncertainty in the current environment. Both downward and upward revisions can happen with respect to governments' financing requirements in the course of the year, which may lead to further changes in the planned issuing activities. In cases where DMOs refrain from announcing a detailed issuance plan for the coming periods, this should be clearly communicated as an exceptional (and temporary) practice.

Furthermore, a combination of a surge in funding needs with adverse market conditions might result in less successful auctions. Even if these are rare market events, they can create market noise. Maintaining a strong two-way communication policy with investors and intermediaries such as primary dealers, rating agencies and other government departments, are instrumental in reducing the type of market noise that can unnecessarily spur borrowing costs. A well designed communication strategy enables debt management offices to i) ensure awareness of fiscal, economic and debt management developments; ii) gauge investor appetite, grasp investment trends and obtain feedback on investor needs, and iii) provide investors with the information they need on a timely basis including changes in auction dates or new issuance.

In light of the growing importance of online communication during the pandemic, sovereign issuers should use electronic communication tools to disseminate information. For example, public announcements disseminated via emails, websites and social media accounts can be quite effective in reaching out to all types of investors including retail investors.

3.6. Role of contingency tools to weather the storm

Liquidity management is critical to enable the government to meet its extended obligations during the pandemic. Borrowing conditions for sovereign issuers can become extremely challenging when rising funding pressures coincide with sudden shifts in market sentiment to a more risk averse mood and deteriorations in perceptions of sovereign risk. In this regard, some level of flexibility is necessary to provide issuers with room for manoeuvre in financing plans. Country experiences suggest that the availability of contingency funding tools, which provide flexibility for issuance plans, is critical for confronting challenges in periods of market stress (OECD, 2019[3])). Today, the role of flexibility in issuance programmes has become more important given the uncertainty associated with control of the pandemic, and governments' borrowing needs. In addition to providing flexibility, putting contingency funding plans into practice would also help to boost market confidence in governments' ability to repay debt as well as respond the pandemic. This is, in particular, relevant for the countries with high redemption profiles and limited access to deep financial markets.

Over the last decade, many governments have established contingency funding tools in case of a significant increase in borrowing needs. If not pre-established, DMOs should develop appropriate contingency funding plans where needed. Commonly used contingency funding sources are:

- immediate access to asset portfolio/liquidity buffer
    - issuance of short-term instruments, such as T-Bills and commercial paper;
    - increase auction size and tap existing bonds
- hold syndications and private placements
- establish overdraft facility arrangements with CBs, and
- set-up credit lines with commercial banks

One of the most commonly used contingency funding tools is a liquidity buffer (LB) policy, which provides DMOs with an immediate access to cash (Box 3.2). Keeping a liquidity buffer cushions event risks and increases financial flexibility to the extent of its availability. In view of the pandemic, DMOs can recalibrate cash buffers to provide additional flexibility. It is important to note that during the crisis, reducing funding risk should take priority over concerns about containing costs. One way of building up cash buffers is to increase auction size and tap existing bonds, another one is to issue short-term securities in markets. Building additional flexibility, such as boosting cash reserves, providing flexibility at auctions, and allowing in-year adjustments to the issuance calendar, will help governments to withstand surges in additional funding needs until long-term financing can be secured.

During the crisis, issuance methods other than auctions would be useful in raising liquidity. Holding syndications for example, helps to retain flexibility in aligning demand with supply as each syndication is sized taking into account the size and quality of end-investor demand. Similarly, private placements, which can be arranged at short notice, are useful for supporting issuance programmes.

The magnitude of the changes in borrowing needs and market conditions will largely depend on recovery of the global economy and how the outbreak evolves, both of which remain highly uncertain. Given the significant amount of uncertainty, sovereign issuers should prepare for longer term disruptions in view of potential increases in liquidity needs. As discussed, they can issue T-bills to build up cash buffers, or look for alternative financing sources, such as additional credit lines with commercial banks, or tapping institutional investors (e.g. foreign or domestic pension funds, insurance companies) through private placements. In addition, temporary arrangements with other government entities can be made so that idle liquid assets available to other government bodies can be withdrawn in the case of emergency. Lastly, when borrowing from other sources becomes unreasonable or inadequate (or impossible), governments should consider financing assistance from bilateral and multilateral resources (e.g. the IMF and the World Bank).

Box 3.2. Liquidity buffer practices of sovereign debt management offices in the OECD area

A cash buffer policy is a liquidity management plan aimed at having cash-like financial assets readily available to address liquidity and refunding risks associated with governments' budget execution and debt management. It is used to manage differences between cash inflows and outflows, and to address short-term loss of market access due to operational issues (e.g. a natural disaster, a cyber-attack or terror attack may hinder auctioning debt).

Keeping a LB has become a widespread practice amongst DMOs in OECD countries over the last decade. A 2017 survey on LB practices amongst the member of the OECD Working Party on Debt Management revealed that 28 DMOs including Canada, Denmark, France, Italy, Portugal, Turkey and the United States maintain a LB as a precautionary measure for extraordinary periods. The survey indicates that the level of cash buffer varies significantly amongst respondent DMOs. They keep cash buffer levels ranging from 5 days to one year of total outlays, including debt payments. Although levels are variable across countries, the most common buffer level is sufficient to meet one month of debt redemptions on average.

The minimum level of LBs depends on various factors such as access to liquid markets, gross borrowing needs and potential funding risks in coming periods. Ideally, the level should be sufficient to meet financing needs during periods of liquidity strains, while taking the cost of keeping idle cash into account. In general, countries adjust the level in order to cover financing obligations for a certain period of time (e.g. survival period) or for a certain percentage of debt.

Over time, the policy regarding the minimum level of liquidity buffer is adjusted to the evolving market structures and changing financing needs. For example, when there is an expected event that might have an impact on borrowing needs or market conditions, a debt management office might benefit from building up the buffer beforehand to provide additional flexibility. This would also help to boost investors' confidence.

An important aspect of cash buffer practices is the need for close coordination amongst relevant authorities as generally, several entities are involved in government cash management operations. It requires a timely flow of information on budget and cash flow projections between the ministry of finance and debt management team. Similarly, coordination is necessary between the central bank and DMO, as most governments keep their cash buffers in their accounts at national central banks. This is a common practice in view of credit risk considerations.

References

Cruz, P. and F. Koc (2018), "The liquidity buffer practices of public debt managers in OECD countries", *OECD Working Papers on Sovereign Borrowing and Public Debt Management*, Vol. No. 9, http://dx.doi.org/10.1887/3b468966-en. [5]

Hurcan, Y., F. Koc and E. Balibek (2020), "How to set up a cash buffer: A practical guide to develop and implement a cash buffer policy". [6]

OECD (2020), *OECD Economic Outlook, Volume 2020 Issue 1: Preliminary version*, OECD Publishing, Paris, https://dx.doi.org/10.1787/0d1d1e2e-en. [1]

OECD (2019), *OECD Sovereign Borrowing Outlook 2019*, OECD Publishing, [3]
https://doi.org/10.1787/aa7aad38-en.

OECD (2018), *OECD Sovereign Borrowing Outlook 2018*, OECD Publishing, [4]
https://doi.org/10.1787/23060476.

OECD (2016), *OECD Sovereign Borrowing Outlook 2016*, OECD Publishing, Paris, [2]
https://dx.doi.org/10.1787/sov_b_outlk-2016-en.

Notes

[1] In the OECD area, cash and debt management functions are mostly integrated. If not integrated, cash and debt management should be closely coordinated.

[2] The ways-and means facility is the government's overdraft account with the BoE and provides the government with cash advances from the BoE. The government usually uses this facility to finance its day-to-day spending, before the BoEs sells government bonds to the market. This facility is normally capped at GBP 370 million. See press releases from HM Treasury here, and BoE here.

[3] The World Health Organisation (WHO) declared COVID-19 a pandemic on March 11, 2020. https://www.who.int/dg/speeches/detail/who-director-general-s-opening-remarks-at-the-media-briefing-on-covid-19---11-march-2020

[4] A post-auction option facility or non-competitive subscription gives successful bidders the option to purchase an additional amount allocated to them at a particular auction. Its price is based on the average price of all competitive bids submitted.

[5] As market makers, banks act as both agency traders to match buyers and sellers, and as principal traders stepping in to buy and sell securities on behalf of clients using their own balance sheets. Hence, primary dealer banks are seen as reliable liquidity providers. However, more stringent rules on capital requirements following the GFC have made banks less willing to act as intermediaries by providing so-called warehouse of risk, instead looking to connect buyers and sellers immediately.

[6] A predictable issuance programme: i) raises DMO's credibility, accountability; ii) allows transparent allocation; iii) reduces uncertainty for investors; iv) facilitates better communication and marketing. This, in turn, – based on expert judgment and investors' feedback – broadens the investor base, lowers risk premiums and decreases borrowing costs and fosters secondary market liquidity.

www.ingramcontent.com/pod-product-compliance
Lightning Source LLC
Chambersburg PA
CBHW081202270326
41930CB00014B/3269